UPRIVER AND DOWNSTREAM

UPRIVER AND DOWNSTREAM

THE BEST FLY-FISHING AND ANGLING ADVENTURES FROM THE *New York Times*

Edited by Stephen Sautner

Introduction by Verlyn Klinkenborg

Illustrations by Glenn Wolff

THREE RIVERS PRESS

NEW YORK

Originally published in hardcover in the United States by Harmony Books,
an imprint of the Crown Publishing Group, a division of
Random House, Inc., New York, in 2007.

Grateful acknowledgment is made to Alfred A. Knopf for permission to reprint
an excerpt from *The Longest Silence: A Life in Fishing* by Thomas McGuane.
Copyright © 1999 by Thomas McGuane. Reprinted by permission of
Alfred A. Knopf, a division of Random House, Inc.

Library of Congress Cataloging-in-Publication Data
Upriver and downstream : the best fly-fishing and angling adventures from
the *New York Times* / edited by Stephen Sautner ; introduction by Verlyn
Klinkenborg ; illustrations by Glenn Wolff. — 1st ed.
1. Fly fishing.   I. Sautner, Stephen.
SH456.U67 2007
799.12'4 — dc22   2006037397

ISBN 978-0-307-38259-7

Printed in the United States of America

Design by Leonard Henderson

10 9 8 7 6 5 4 3 2 1

First Paperback Edition

"Gee but that's fun. Don't that pole of your'n bend!"

— Ray Bergman, *Just Fishing*, 1932

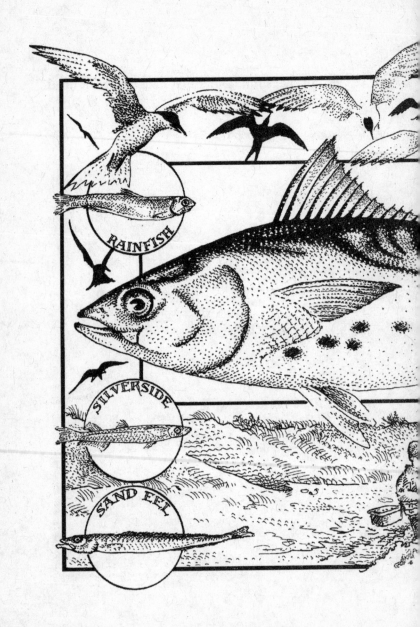

RAINFISH

SILVERSIDE

SAND EEL

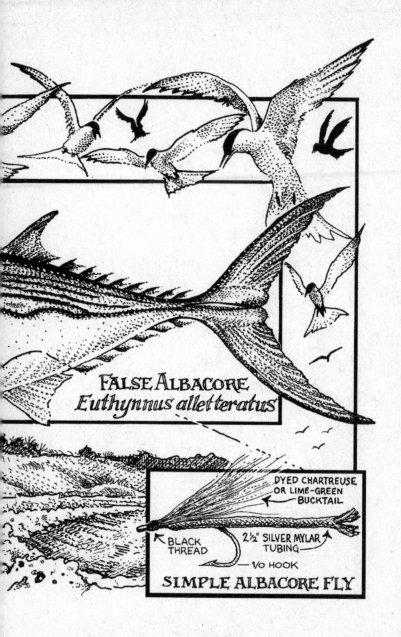

FALSE ALBACORE
Euthynnus alletteratus

DYED CHARTREUSE
OR LIME-GREEN
BUCKTAIL

BLACK
THREAD

2½" SILVER MYLAR
TUBING

1/0 HOOK

SIMPLE ALBACORE FLY

CONTENTS

xvii Editor's Note

xix Introduction by Verlyn Klinkenborg

1 **COLDWATERS**

3 *Following a Fluid Trail Even Higher*
BY NICK LYONS

6 *A Presence at the Source of the Noble Brookie*
BY PETE BODO

9 *The Wisdom of* The Compleat Angler *at 350*
BY VERLYN KLINKENBORG

12 *A Little Cold and Wet Is Fine for Spring's Cornucopia*
BY ERNEST SCHWIEBERT

17 *Sometimes, Taming a Horse Seems Easier*
BY STEPHEN SAUTNER

21 *Getting Cold and Wet Proves Worth the Effort*
BY PETER KAMINSKY

24 *Drawn to a Wild, Remote River*
BY NELSON BRYANT

28 *Aliens in the Delaware Are Welcome to Stay*
BY PETE BODO

31 *Of Fallen Fruit and Fanciful Fishing*
BY NELSON BRYANT

35 *Manhattan as a Paradise for Trout and Fly-Fishing*
BY NICHOLAS KARAS

38 *A Trout Tryst: Waiting for You Is the Big One*
BY PATRICIA LEIGH BROWN

43 *Trumping Rules of a Private Paradise*
BY JOHN van VLIET

48 *Tapping Plump Browns, with a Bayou Nymph*
BY ADAM CLYMER

51 *Finding a Little Paradise in Fishing the Tailwaters*
BY PETER KAMINSKY

54 *Wyoming Rivers Produce Trophies*
BY GREG THOMAS

58 *Of Gleaming Trout and Undying Friendship*
BY NELSON BRYANT

62 *Returning to the Pure and Simple Joys of Fishing*
BY PETE BODO

65 *Savoring a Salmon Holding Pool*
BY NELSON BRYANT

69 *Good Alaska Fishing Comes with Time*
BY STEPHEN SAUTNER

73 *A Steelhead Challenge in the British Columbia Wilderness*
BY THOMAS McGUANE

77 *A Meditation on the Fly-Fisher in Winter*
BY ERNEST SCHWIEBERT

81 **WARMWATERS**

83 *Season of the Bigmouth Approaches*
BY NICK LYONS

87 *As the Season Gets Colder, the Bass Get Wiser*
BY ROBERT H. BOYLE

90 *Struggling to Master a New Fishing Language*
BY JAMES GORMAN

94 *In the Depths of Central Park, Fishing on the Fly*
BY PAUL GUERNSEY

97 *Smallmouth Bass Help in Ending a Brief Slump*
BY JAMES GORMAN

101 *Nature Has a Way of Finding Us All*

BY CRAIG SPRINGER

104 *Letting Nature Work, with Aid from an Earthmover*

BY NICK LYONS

108 *Looking for Pickerel and Renewing Life at Camp*

BY NELSON BRYANT

112 *A Skinny Little Girl, a Fishing Rod, a Bluegill*

BY NICK LYONS

115 **SALTWATERS**

117 *Casting into the Past for Striped Bass Heaven*

BY C. J. CHIVERS

121 *A Glorious Show of Striped Bass Without a Catch*

BY NICK LYONS

124 *Blitzes Are the Great Hatches of the Sea for Anglers*

BY JOHN WALDMAN

129 *The Special Tests of Playing Fishing Guide*

BY NELSON BRYANT

133 *A Stealthy Pursuit of the Striped Bass*

BY PETER KAMINSKY

136 *Testing a Hypothesis on Time and River Fishing*

BY JAMES GORMAN

140 *Playing Hide-and-Seek with the Monster Bluefish*
BY PETE BODO

144 *As You Cast, Watch Out for Low-Flying Planes*
BY STEPHEN SAUTNER

148 *Cape Cod Beauty Seen Even Before* Mayflower
BY MARGOT PAGE

152 *Seeking Reassurance, and Finding It in Fishing*
BY PETE BODO

156 *A Familiar Old Pond Still Brings Surprises*
BY NELSON BRYANT

160 *A Young Angler's Introduction to the Food Chain*
BY PETER KAMINSKY

164 *Anglers in Search of False Albacore*
BY STEPHEN SAUTNER

167 *Is This Albacore Heaven? No, It's Just the Outer Banks*
BY PETER KAMINSKY

170 *Baby Tarpon Provide Everglades Challenge*
BY STEPHEN SAUTNER

175 **ODD WATERS**

177 *In Defense of Fishing Winter's Frozen Ponds*
BY JOHN WALDMAN

180 *Looking for a Good Fight? Go Looking for a Carp*
BY BOB BUTZ

183 *Looking for Shad with the Roar of Eighteen-Wheelers Nearby*
BY STEPHEN SAUTNER

186 *Cold Months Bring a Fish a Grandfather Could Love*
BY DAVE TAFT

190 *Spinefish Aplenty in Waters of the East*
BY RAY OTTULICH

193 *From the Cretaceous to a Pan Near You*
BY C. J. CHIVERS

197 *Do Not Be Alarmed; It's Only a Paddlefish*
BY GREG THOMAS

201 *The Lofty Mystery of Why Sturgeon Leap*
BY JOHN WALDMAN

205 *When Fish Came to the Fisherman*
BY STEPHEN SAUTNER

209 *Growing Up in Brooklyn, Feeling at Home in Alaska*
BY DAVE TAFT

213 *Salted Version of Fly-Fishing Is a Hit*
BY ROBERT H. BOYLE

216 *A Feast of Whitebait Begins with a Cast Net*
BY NELSON BRYANT

219 *Late-Summer Ritual: Crabbing on the Hudson*
BY JAMES GORMAN

223 **FAR WATERS**

225 *When Fly-Fishing in England, Please Use Protocol*
BY NICHOLAS KARAS

229 *Fish Stories, Told with a Brogue*
BY BARBARA LLOYD

232 *Salmon and Sea Trout in Reykjavik's Suburbs*
BY JOHN WALDMAN

236 *Pass the Eel, Pass the Vodka, and Carry on a Tradition*
BY JAMES PROSEK

240 *A Week of Highs and Lows at the End of the Earth*
BY PETER KAMINSKY

244 *Fishing Among the Falklands' Shipwrecks*
BY STEPHEN SAUTNER

249 *Where Trout Are Bigger Than the Tallest of Tales*
BY PETER KAMINSKY

253 *Fishing into the Teeth of the Amazon*
BY STEPHEN SAUTNER

256 *In Remote North of Canada, It's a Pike-Eat-Pike Existence*
BY KEN SCHULTZ

260 *Standing on a Mountaintop, Casting for Bonefish*

BY STEPHEN SAUTNER

264 *In Ukraine, Exploring the Riches of the Dnieper*

BY JOHN WALDMAN

269 About the Contributors

275 Acknowledgments

EDITOR'S NOTE

SINCE BEFORE WORLD WAR II, the *New York Times* has dedicated a column to hunting and fishing, originally calling it "Wood, Field and Stream." By the mid-1970s, perhaps to reflect a transformation in both the sporting and physical landscapes, the column had changed names to the less woodsy but more encompassing "Outdoors."

There have been precisely four full-time columnists since 1937. Raymond Camp wrote until 1956 before taking a job in the Bahamas. Former *Times* photo editor John Randolph then held the job until his death in 1961. After Randolph, Oscar Godbout wrote the column before dying of a heart attack in 1967 at age forty. Then came the indefatigable Nelson Bryant, who assumed the helm after giving up a job as a dock builder. Though he officially retired in 1991 at age sixty-eight, he still contributed freelance stories from his home on Martha's Vineyard until 2006.

When Bryant stepped down as a full-time columnist, the *Times* began to draw from a bullpen of eager freelancers. Added to the mix were a few veteran *Times* staff reporters who took breathers from their normal beats of national politics, New York City crime, or the heady world of hard science to contribute an occasional ode to striped bass or Midwestern trout. Suddenly a column that went from four writers over half a century exploded to dozens of contributors from all over the United States and beyond. This collection reflects this particularly exhilarating period in the column's history.

Even so, "Outdoors" will always remain in the shadows of the Big Four sports — not to mention burgeoning "growth sports" like NASCAR and Major League Soccer. It reminds me of a secret native brook trout stream in New Jersey that's sandwiched between a strip mall and a used-car dealership. The fish are there, but you have to bushwhack to get them. Still, seventy years later, it's good to know that you can pick up a *New York Times* and, on the right day, read about ice fishing with maggots by John Waldman, or discover the joys of catching sea-herring from a pier in Brooklyn in a piece by Dave Taft. Like the native trout stream, you can still find something prized, like those little brookies that dart about in hidden waters.

— *Stephen Sautner*

INTRODUCTION

I WRITE EDITORIALS for the *New York Times*, which means that sometimes people who read editorials write to me. Many of the letters are kind and thoughtful. But whenever I write something less than serious, there is always a vein of criticism that goes like this: "In such a grim world," the reader wonders, "how can you waste such valuable space on such frivolity?" That is another way of asking, in reference to the book you now hold in your hands, "What has the *New York Times* got to do with fishing?"

I take it for granted that fishing — personal fishing — is serious stuff and that, at the same time, it doesn't belong above the fold on the front page of the *Times*. There is no news in fishing, or rather there's always the same old good news. Any angler worth the name has long since learned to pretend that what matters is the angling, not the catching, so even landing the big one that lives under the bridge isn't really news. It's just part of the smooth, even temper of this most philosophical of sports.

Over the years, fishing has been found all over the newspaper, but it turns up most often in the sports pages. The principle, I take it, is that since baseball players have been known to go bass-fishing in the off-season, the sports pages are where fishing belongs. Because every angler worth the name knows enough to pretend that fishing is not a competitive sport.

Fishing crops up in the *Times* partly as a branch of natural history and partly, of course, because there are some devoted anglers among the men and women who write for the paper and those who read it. These essays about fishing — bluefish in the Hamptons, piranha in the Amazon, brown trout in the Catskills — also help leaven the hard news. You begin to understand the special place fishing occupies in the *Times* when you realize that there is no equivalent golf column.

But I think these fishing pieces add something else to the reader's experience of the paper, something no less tangible even when you read them here, in a different context. A newspaper records the broad range of human events but with a narrow emotional amplitude. Its language is explicit, never tacit. It abhors implication and distrusts irony. It expresses empathy only within sobering limits. It has almost nothing to say about the darkness of cynicism and disbelief or the possibilities of joy and love. The newspaper is a chronicle of human existence, but the humans who appear in it nearly always lack the fullness of their humanity. They are subordinate to history itself. They are sources, victims, subjects, examples, authorities, officials, spokespersons, reporters — partial selves, in other words.

But something is different in these fishing essays. It's as though the humans we watch here — hip-deep in a spring freshet, calf-deep on a bonefish flat — come closer to being the whole person. This isn't just a rhetorical flourish, a handy journalistic device. It reflects the genuine feel of fishing. You spend the day in the tug of moving water. You fight the sun's glare and the wind that eats your backcast. You cast to shadows — a permit ghosting away or the silhouette of a feeding rainbow just at dark. And nearly all of what is inessential about you drifts away.

Good reporters get used to putting a part of themselves

up on the shelf, out of reach, while they're working. It's how the job gets done. The same is true for the rest of us, in different ways. Most of what the working day offers us — most days, that is — doesn't exactly require the fullness of our being, and so we live partially, economically. You'd think that the effort needed to fish well — to cast precisely, to notice all the things that need noticing — would require an even thinner slice of ourselves. But that isn't the way it works. We focus intently. A lighter tippet. A smaller fly. A cleaner drift. Hour after hour. And it is the focus that frees us to be a little bit larger than we usually get to be.

You can draw all sorts of analogies between fishing and life, if you like. But you'll notice that the writers here don't do much of that. If you're fishing analogically, you're not really fishing. Most of us go fishing not to observe the way it resembles the nature of life but to immerse ourselves in a life that asks us only to pay attention. And so we pay attention to what is happening out there — in the deep, in the shallows, at the end of the line — and discover, strangely enough, how much play our emotions get in the course of the day. Not just the feelings that come with stalking and hooking and witnessing the fish but those vastly subtler, almost iridescent emotions that come and go as quick as thought.

Don't get me wrong. This is a collection of tough minds at play. These people are not weeping as they angle, nor are they laughing aloud. They barely admit, most of them, what I've been talking about here. But the beauty of these essays, apart from the fishing itself, is that they don't mind irony and they don't fear implication. A greater fraction of the whole person shows up in these essays than almost anywhere else in the newspaper, reminding us — those of us who fish, at least — of the greater fraction we get to be when we're out on the lake or the river or the ocean.

Sooner or later, the fishing trip comes to an end, and we

go back to ordinary life. That is very much how these essays worked when they first appeared one by one in the *Times*. No matter how slowly you read them, they were soon engulfed by the rest of the day's news. That is the beauty of having them in a book. All the news has been pared away. The editorials, too.

—*Verlyn Klinkenborg*

UPRIVER AND DOWNSTREAM

COLDWATERS

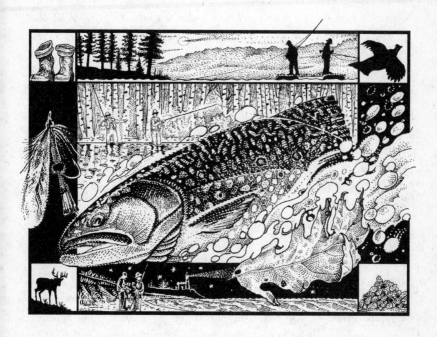

Though an official tally has never been taken, trout and salmon have dominated "Outdoors" columns from the beginning. The reason why is simple: anglers still can't figure out how to catch them, and need to explain themselves. Brown trout leisurely gulp mayflies for hours, eating what seems like every bug on the river—except the fly you painstakingly crafted to imitate each leg, wing, and antenna of the real thing. A twenty-five-pound Atlantic salmon continually rises at the tail-out of a slow pool, wags its tail once or twice, then glides back to its lie. Once—and only once—the salmon tilts its massive body upward for an extra second to consider with its pea-brain a fly you just cast three hundred times. Later, as the sun is setting, you reel up your line and declare, "It was a good day . . . I rose one."

Clearly this demands justification. Those who have never spent eleven hours on a trout stream or salmon river want facts. "How can you stand there all day long and not catch anything?" they ask.

So you clear your throat and begin: "Well, you see, it was the barometer." Or the water was too high, or too low, or too cold, or warm, or it turns out that Ephemerella cornutella was hatching and you mistakenly thought it was Isonychia sadleri, or the dog ate your waders. By this time your interrogator's eyes have long since glazed over—or perhaps even shut completely.

But some know that trout and salmon happen to live in some of the most heartbreakingly beautiful places on the planet. This smaller group needs less of an explanation than a reaffirmation. They want to smell hemlocks again. They need to feel river mud squishing under the felt soles of their waders. They long to hear a hermit thrush singing just before the first bats of the night appear above a riffle. They nod know-ingly and understand. To them, you don't need to explain a thing, but they relish every word nonetheless.

FOLLOWING A FLUID TRAIL

EVEN HIGHER

By Nick Lyons

I
T IS WINTER when I turn on the faucet; despite the
ice and snow, water flows easily for as long as I like,
ending its cold trip from wildness to what we call civilization. I watch for a moment, stunned by this rush of clear
liquid I've seen ten thousand times before, then twist the
faucet until the flow diminishes and stops. The water may
have begun on some remote hillside, but it has come directly
from a city reservoir not a mile from my apartment or one no
more than twenty miles upcountry.

I once fished in such a nearby body of water, unceremoniously called "Reservoir 3," chiefly because friends from
Brooklyn had it on good authority that the Canadian exhibit at
the old Madison Square Garden Sportsman's Show dumped
their Atlantic salmon and ouananiche (pronounced wah-
NAH-nish) there. We were mad to catch ouananiche.

We had seen them at the show — long, brilliantly spotted,
with a bright reddish hue. There was something magical, exotic, about their name. We had been bred on silvery trout,
fresh from a hatchery, and these creatures absolutely exuded
wildness. We tried desperately, fruitlessly, for three years to
extract even one from Reservoir 3 — and in the end we had to
settle for messes of crappie.

If you follow the liquid trail beyond such reservoirs — usually north, often joined by canals, pipeways, sluices of man-made rivers to other reservoirs — you will find that in each, successively, the water is colder, the fish more beautiful. Crappie, bluegill, and perch give way to smallmouth bass, which, in turn, at higher elevations, become brown and rainbow trout.

The reservoirs, man-made, can provide fine sport, and so can the various waterways between them. In one such river, fed by one reservoir and running only three miles into another, I did most of my early trout fishing. It did not feel artificial to me. I was a city kid and almost all flowing water was manna then; and the trout, mostly stocked a few weeks earlier, for years brought us excitement — especially when we took a larger fish, one held over from the previous season. But we caught no ouananiche.

Above the last reservoir, something else happens: the water is colder, wilder, mysterious. In one headwaters creek I know, high in the Catskills, the gradient steep and riffles thin, everything is untouched by civilization. There was logging here a hundred years ago; telephone wires connect a remote wildlife manager's cabin to the nearest town; now and again some kids walk in, leaving their bikes three miles below. It's wilderness, all right — as good as you'll find this side of Labrador.

In spring spate, the river rises ten feet and takes everything in its path; in high summer, its flow oozes between exposed boulders and becomes as clear as water from the tap. The place is overhung with hemlock, willow, and birch, so that the alley of the river is intimate, shady. I have walked up there, skipping from stone to stone when the summer heat is up, in sneakers, looking for pockets large enough to hold a trout or two.

There are such pools and runs and undercut banks, and a

dry fly pitched into them will bring a quick, eager spurt of water. These trout are not selective feeders; they are thorough-going opportunists and will take a Christmastree of a Royal Coachman as quickly as they'll take a fallen ant. Once I saw a big yellow stonefly fluttering over one of the larger pools, switched to a No. 6 Stimulator, and caught a ten-incher, a prize in these small waters.

These are wild brook trout — five, six, sometimes eight inches, on rare occasions a foot long. They have flanks as smooth as an otter's skin, a dark mottled back, rose marks the color of wild strawberries, and striped fins. They wiggle like live jewels when you hoist them out of the water.

Greedy and wanton to their near extinction, vulnerable, full of a wildness that cannot protect itself, these fish are the ultimate symbol of piscatorial wildness, and it delights me to catch a dozen on barbless hooks and slip them swiftly back into their element. When I first climbed to the fountainhead of all city water and saw them, I stopped thinking of exotic Canadian fish and knew I had found a quiet place that satisfied all my longings.

Little do these diminutive flashes of light and color know the fate, downriver, of the precious, pure liquid in which they flourish. Little do they care — so long as it is there, so long as the great cities do not drink them into extinction. They are beautiful, rare creatures that dance in my head and I think of them even now, in the dead of winter, every time I turn on and turn off the faucet. *(February 22, 1996)*

A PRESENCE AT THE SOURCE

OF THE NOBLE BROOKIE

BY PETE BODO

ANDES, N.Y. — The water swirling gently at the base of the muscular willow crowding the brook was the color of pea soup, and so deep that the bottom was invisible — a feature so dramatic on this small ribbon of water that it qualified as an authentic "honey hole." This is the angler's catchphrase for one of those rare, reliable places that always hold fish but are usually surrounded by a few opportunistic nimrods as well.

But this time it was different. Although it was an ideal afternoon for fishing in the Catskills, whose proliferation of valleys and hollows formed the original cradle of United States fly-fishing, the only other angler on the entire eight-mile length of this tributary to the Pepacton Reservoir was my friend and fishing companion Glyn Vincent. Another friend, Jean Kormos, a Manhattan tailor, had joined us as well, but only to study the elaborate stitching in the leaves of various riparian plants.

We were fishing on one of those warm, sunshot days of spring — a time when lime-green skunk cabbage shoots up through the leaf fodder and seems to bloom right before your eyes — on the retired farm of Bob and Francis Stevens.

Although absent, Bob was ably represented by the family's adorable but coyote-shy dog, a shepherd mix named Belle. She enthusiastically romped along the hay meadow at the edge of the brook, proudly toting whatever object had last caught her attention, including at one point a rusted old Genesee beer can. This is, after all, the ungentrified side of the Catskills.

❖   ❖   ❖

A flicker of gold at the shallow edge of the honey hole, a spooked trout, got me all juiced up. Honey holes are reliable because long after the robust flows of spring subside, they offer trout cool refuge and an acceptable volume of water.

Brooks are the capillaries that feed the arteries, or streams, that become the veins, or rivers, in the complex body of a watershed. They are usually lovely and always fragile environments: the aquatic counterparts of Fabergé eggs. They are at their best from April through May, impetuously tumbling over boulders, rushing through hemlock-shaded gorges, and sliding along undercut banks, drawing volume from snowmelt and spring runs leaching out copious amounts of groundwater.

Come summer, a brook becomes a shadow of its former self and a place of considerable mystery. Its cold waters, reduced to a mere trickle, often disappear for long stretches into the labyrinth of underground channels gouged out by heavy water in better times. Researchers at Penn State University have found that at the peak of summer, some trout will go underground, as it were, to survive. It's a touching thought, and thankfully nobody harasses the fish in that difficult period.

In fact, few people bother to fish brooks at all, at any time, and those most inclined to look down their noses at brooks are avid fly-fishers. The appeal of brooks is diminished by their diminutive size. You have to walk, scramble, and climb, often far from the road, to fish them. You rarely get to cast in any meaningful sense on a brook. The paucity of food in most brooks makes the trout indiscriminate, so you can throw all of that matching-the-hatch mumbo-jumbo right out the window. And the movie version of the angling experience in brooks would probably be called *Honey, I Shrunk the Trout*.

But brook fish are tiny bundles of glory, with a noble tale to tell. They represent the last vestiges of the only trout indigenous to the Catskills, the eastern brook trout, a jewel of a fish with an olive back, orange and yellow spots, and elegant, ivory-edged fins. "Brookies" can exist only in the purest and coldest of waters, and the stocks of these fish, in literally hundreds of miles of small waters, are not only living reminders of a despoiled natural heritage, but also as indigenous, wild fish they remind us of who we are and where we came from. They are the ghosts in the industrial-age fishing-for-recreation machine.

I looked upstream, just in time to see Glyn flick his rod upward. A six-inch brookie flashed in the sunlight, and fell back into the brook, free. I returned to my own problem. Fishing a brook can be maddening, in the same way as changing clothing in a telephone booth is for anyone except Superman. I had to figure out a way to drop and direct a weighted bead-head nymph into the honey hole by poking my rod tip through the budding pussy willows and alders guarding it.

On three successive attempts, the fly got entangled in the brush or wrapped around the overhead boughs. Honey holes may be reliable, but they aren't always easy. While I was unmaking my last mess, with the rod resting on the bank behind me, Belle got her legs entangled in my fly line and spooked. I heard the tip snap off. The dog returned, with her tongue hanging out and a goofy, apologetic grin on her face.

The rod was worth a few hundred bucks, but the experience of fishing a small brook again was not merely frustrating, it was priceless. *(April 30, 2000)*

THE WISDOM OF *THE COMPLEAT*
ANGLER AT 350

By Verlyn Klinkenborg

O NLY A HANDFUL of the books first published in London in the sober year of 1653 are still read today, even by scholars. And only one of that year's first editions has gone on, over the next three and a half centuries, to be reprinted again and again and to find new readers every year.

That book is Izaak Walton's *The Compleat Angler; or, The Contemplative Man's Recreation: Being a Discourse of Fish and Fishing, Not Unworthy the Perusal of Most Anglers.*

There is hardly any assessing how different our world is from Walton's. From today's perspective, 1653 looks like a vastly simpler time, if only because "there were fewer lawyers," as Walton puts it. But simplicity is always deceiving. *The Compleat Angler* was published just four years after England had beheaded its king and brought civil war to an end under the Puritan rule of Oliver Cromwell.

Yet what Walton asks is simply this: "Is it not an art to deceive a Trout with an artificial Fly?" He asks it not as a scholar of angling, sitting in a musty room filled with old books and tackle, but in the persona of Piscator, the fisherman, who teaches Venator, the hunter, how to fish during a beautiful outing in May. And what makes Walton interesting even now is that the art of being an angler was far more complex in his day than it is in ours.

Walton's kind of fisherman had to be able to discourse on Pliny and to quote St. Augustine and to consider the analogies between his art and that of the fishers of men who were called Apostles.

His angler needed to be able to sing as well as bait a hook or tie a fly. He should revel in the pleasures of the countryside and the companionship of other anglers. Venator soon qualifies as a fisherman not just because he catches fish but also because he has a genuine delicacy of soul.

"Let's go to that house," Venator says at the end of the day, "for the linen looks white, and smells of lavender, and I long to lie in a pair of sheets that smell so." If, to us, Piscator sounds didactic and a little long-winded — praising water, for instance, because it allows the English to travel easily to Rome — Venator's patience is only magnified as a result.

It is indeed an art to deceive a trout with an artificial fly, now as well as then. But by "art" Walton means something much more inclusive than technique. As the two men walk along in the shade of a honeysuckle hedge, Piscator turns from the technical matter of painting a fly rod to a question of much greater importance: thankfulness. Fishing may be a contemplative person's recreation, but it's even more fitting for a person who has also taught himself to be thankful. Piscator's byword, in a world full of suffering, is simply this: "Every misery that I miss is a new mercy."

To tie your own flies, gather your own bait, make your own tackle, to sing well, to quote learnedly, to know the seasons of the trout and which winds are preferable for fishing, to love the scent of lavender in an ale-house window, to fish thankfully — these are just the beginnings of the angler's duties, in Walton's eyes. He lived in a time when a fisherman might hate otters, still common then, for destroying trout. But even Walton knew that the love of his sport meant, first of all, a care for nature, which we believe too often, at our peril, can take care of itself. "I remember," he wrote, "that a wise friend of mine did usually say, 'That which is everybody's business is nobody's business.'" Our business, after all this time has passed, is still to learn from Walton. *(May 24, 2003)*

A LITTLE COLD AND WET IS FINE

FOR SPRING'S CORNUCOPIA

By Ernest Schwiebert

THINGS SOMETIMES COME together in moments of tranquillity, and small epiphanies seem unusually welcome these days. I watched with a sense of wonder as a mature doe dropped a fawn beside a dead tree felled in a winter storm, less than thirty yards behind the house.

The doe has been a regular pilgrim in recent years, foraging patiently in our woods, and resting in the sun among the boulders. It was early and rather cool, and the doe had quietly anticipated her calving time in a sheltered place exposed to the morning sun.

Her breakfast miracle was a translucent sac that seemed to enclose a loose bundle of kindling, but it stirred and moved, until the fawn's gangling legs worked free. It seemed all wetness and spindle-leggedness at first, unable to raise itself, its spotted pelt slippery with mucus and blood. It tried to stand and failed. Its tiny head was high, and it struggled to stand, only to collapse like a house of cards, as its mother began to wash it vigorously. Its efforts to walk were comic, all legs and no direction, and it seemed wobbly and frail. The mother washed the baby several times. Its ears were up, sampling a universe of unfamiliar sounds. The mother withdrew to rest beside the deadfall, as her fawn explored the strange new place it had unwillingly entered, until it finally settled to doze in the winter leaves.

It was a potsherd of magic.

We have witnessed a green winter in the foothill ridges above Princeton, New Jersey, and this unpredictable spring has remained quixotic and dour. I went fishing again, hoping a premature fawn might be evidence that the season had regained its equilibrium. It was a warm morning, with no wind and few clouds, but it had been 34 degrees during the night.

❖   ❖   ❖

Brodhead Creek, in northeast Pennsylvania, proved surprisingly void, 45 degrees when I started to fish, and my toes soon ached. But its temperature had climbed to 58 before I finally started home. I had caught and released seven trout, but had captured them with too many flies to have resolved the minor conundrums at hand.

Fish and aquatic insects have no body temperatures of their own and are at the mercy of stream temperatures to regulate their metabolisms. Neither trout nor aquatic insects cope well with steep variations in barometric pressure and temperature, and neither seem particularly fond of such bright, cloudless days. Most anglers will agree that dull weather, with a steady barometer and veiled in misting rain, is optimal unless it is simply too wintry and raw.

"Why do fish and fly hatches seem to come better with a little rain?" I once asked a boyhood mentor in the Catskills.

"They're already cold and wet," he replied. "They don't mind a little more."

Our Appalachian spring has been late this year, and stream insects usually found emerging had still not appeared last week. Yellow-bodied *Ceratopsyche* sedges have begun to trickle off in modest numbers, but fish are still not taking them well, and the yellow-bodied *Ephemerella* mayflies called Pale Evening Duns have not yet arrived. These are bellwether species that precede the most theatrical aquatic hatches of the trout-fishing year.

Other caddis flies are also important in late spring and early summer. Perhaps the most notable are medium-sized specimens of the green-bodied genus called *Rhyacophila,* and the plentiful slate-winged sedges of the somber *Psilotreta* clan. Old soft-hackled Yorkshire patterns like the Partridge and Green, and the Partridge and Olive, are workable imitations.

But the last few weeks of spring usually surrender a cornucopia of important mayflies, and their hatchings and twilight egg-layings are just cause for celebration.

Few are more important than the closely related genera *Stenonema* and *Stenacron.* These are rather large mayflies with handsome mottled wings, and anglers have given them names like March Brown, Gray Fox, and Light Cahill. The first two seem to emerge sporadically, between late morning and afternoon, in sufficient numbers to trigger rises of trout, and after they have been hatching steadily, fish seem to watch for them. Anglers may fish imitations at random with reasonable success. Light Cahills are mostly evening hatches, and large mating swarms of all three mayflies are typically encountered at twilight.

Other pale *Ephemerella* flies also appear at twilight in late spring, and there is another small species that most anglers describe as the Pale Sulfur. There are morning hatches called Blue Winged Olives, and the primary species involved include *Ephemerella cornuta* and the slightly smaller *Ephemerella cornutella.* The timing of their emergences is governed by air temperatures the night before. Cold nights result in late-morning hatches, while warm nights mean fly-fishers should expect to find the Olives before breakfast. Mating choreography occurs in early evening, and their small blackish-olive spinners usually fall spent at nightfall.

Perhaps the most theatrical Eastern hatch is the large

mayfly that fly-fishers call the Green Drake. Its taxonomic name is *Ephemera guttulata,* and it is a unique late-spring species indigenous only to Eastern trout streams.

There is no mistaking Green Drakes on the water or climbing toward the trees through the gathering darkness. Their wings are mottled and olivaceous on mountain fisheries of acidic water chemistry, but are more yellowish and less darkly mottled on the lime-rich streams of central Pennsylvania. Such flies are clearly a mouthful, and even trophy fish relish them.

Freshly hatched specimens molt in the riparian foliage for two to three days, and return utterly transformed. The crystalline wings are rather heavily mottled with ebony, with an olive cast, while the abdomens are chalky white. Anglers call them Coffin Flies. On streams where they are plentiful, twilight mating swarms still gather thick as blizzards. Trout will gorge once these large spinners complete their aerial mating.

Some streams are no longer graced with fishable populations of the Green Drake. The Brodhead once surrendered them in great numbers, and its populations were known for darkly blotched wings of a particularly intense olive. But their burrowing nymphs are found in benthic silts, and both sediment and the Green Drakes were brutally displaced in the summer hurricane flood of 1955. They have never returned in fishable numbers.

Other storied fly hatches appear at the threshold of summer, and no list would be complete without mayflies of the genus *Isonychia.* Their nymphs are fast-water dwellers with the agility of acrobats, hopscotching brashly from stone to stone and traveling in the benthic drift. Some taxonomists say the genetic codes of *Isonychia sadleri* and *Isonychia bicolor* are virtually the same, but knowledgeable anglers know that they differ in size and color and seldom hatch at the same times, and that separate fly patterns are required to imitate them.

Isonychia sadleri is larger and has a dull reddish body, while *Isonychia bicolor* is a dour grayish sepia. The nymphal stages are easily separated. The mature nymphs of *Isonychia sadleri* have a white axial stripe running their entire length, while the nymphs of *Isonychia bicolor* have stripes reaching from their heads to the midpoints of their bodies.

These are important fly hatches of early summer and are most commonly encountered at twilight, with their egg-laying spinners falling at dark. Sporadic emergences of *Isonychia bicolor* will continue throughout the summer, with substantive broods in September, but their principal emergences are obviously concentrated in late spring and early summer.

Such hatches are a prelude to the fullness of summer itself and its doldrums of low water, when aquatic insects and their diurnal timing are completely different, and virtually everything astream will be changed.

The British soldier and poet Rupert Brooke was a fisherman whose generation was decimated in Flanders and on the Somme. He witnessed both war and the bountiful chalk-stream weeks of early summer firsthand, and celebrated its cornucopia of plenty in the poem "Heaven" before his death in 1915.

> *Fish (fly-replete, in depth of June,*
> *Dawdling away their wat'ry noon).*

(June 8, 2003)

SOMETIMES, TAMING A HORSE SEEMS EASIER

By Stephen Sautner

H ANCOCK, N.Y. — It was the kind of day when, if the stars have aligned and you have been especially good, the Fishing Gods will smile and mayflies and caddis flies will hatch all day on the upper Delaware River.

Jim Leedom and I spotted the first rise at ten-thirty, followed by another, and then another. We quickly gathered fishing gear from our campsite, then slid our canoe into the river for a short paddle to the far bank, where the snouts of large trout poked through the surface at the tail-out of a deep pool.

We beached the boat and walked quietly downstream along the grassy shoreline. Small caddis, the size and color of brown rice kernels, danced and skipped along the river. Periodically one would vanish in an audible slurp of a rising trout. Perhaps eight fish had gathered to feed along the tail-out, stationing themselves in various lies.

With several targets to choose from, Jim set up ten yards below me, aiming at a particularly splashy riser. I picked out two fish feeding side by side some forty feet into the main current.

Unlike most trout streams in the East, where a reasonable cast with a reasonable fly often prompts a rise, fishing in the Delaware takes the kind of patience one might associate with cracking a safe. Sometimes it takes a dozen fly changes, lengthening one's leader to cobweb-thin tippet, or even crossing the river for just the right drift to provoke even a look from a fish. Other times, the right combination is never found, and you finally wander away after dark with the sounds of trout still rising and splashing everywhere.

My first few drifts with a size-16 elk-hair caddis went ignored, even though the two trout continued to rise freely. Each fish would come up about every twenty seconds and leisurely suck down another caddis fly, sending rings that seemed to push my own imitations out of the way. Several times, the farther of the two fish porpoised to grab a struggling caddis, revealing the broad, dark back of what was clearly a very large brown trout. By the end of the first half hour of casting vainly to this huge, rising fish, I began calling it the Horse.

Suddenly Jim yelled out, and I glanced downriver to see his rod bent deeply and a big brown in midleap. He chased after it, appearing smaller and smaller as the trout took him farther downstream. Finally, two hundred yards away, he beached the fish, then briefly held it up for me to see. When he returned, he had that glazed, contented look of an angler who had just released a very nice trout. "Twenty inches," he said, almost out of breath. "Took a March Brown."

For the uninitiated, March Browns are meaty mayflies many times larger than caddis.

After I congratulated Jim, I went back to the business at hand. Perhaps the Horse or his smaller cousin (the Pony?) would like a March Brown–sized meal. I quickly snipped off the caddis and tied on a much larger and bushier offering.

To my surprise, on just the second drift, the Horse's sidekick sucked in the fly. I lifted, and the fish flew from the river, then dashed off downstream, taking line. Within a few minutes a butter-yellow, heavily spotted brown measuring seventeen inches lay in my hand.

"Nice trout," Jim said, walking over just as I released it.

Stoically, I looked up and said, "The other one is much bigger." Then we both turned just in time to watch the Horse suck in yet another caddis.

Sensing an Ahab-versus-the-white-whale scenario that anglers sometimes go through, Jim stepped aside as I waded back in, now hunched over like a great blue heron. The songs of warblers, thrushes, and tanagers calling from the surrounding hillsides suddenly faded into little more than muffled background noise. Even a lone bald eagle soaring upriver was worth little more than a halfhearted glance.

But the March Brown didn't work; neither would a smaller caddis, or a caddis emerger, or a March Brown emerger. I lengthened my leader to fifteen feet. I threw slack-line casts and mended line endlessly. The Horse remained unimpressed. Too many casts over it, and it would sometimes stop rising, as if to teach me a lesson. But inevitably it would start coming up a few minutes later, sometimes a yard or two upstream, or perhaps five feet farther into the current. And when it did, I resumed casting.

And so it went into the early afternoon. Jim had long since gone downriver, where he released a few smaller fish. Eventually he returned to find me in the exact same position. "Still working on that trout?" he asked.

At this point I just nodded. My shoulder ached from repeated casting, and the dry patch on my fishing vest began to resemble the bargain bin of a fly shop, with various bedraggled patterns freshly rejected by the Horse hanging in a clump.

By hour three, the caddis hatch began tapering off. Jim suggested we go back to camp, and I agreed. In fishing, as in all sports, you sometimes have to tip your hat to your opponent, even if your opponent has a brain the size of a raisin. We began walking upstream when the Horse rose one more time.

I stopped. Jim understood. I stripped off forty feet of line, false-cast once or twice, then dropped yet another caddis pattern just above the fish's feeding lane. The fly drifted a few feet, then vanished in a slurping rise — just like that.

"I got him," I yelled triumphantly, feeling as if I had just split the atom. But the Horse had other plans. It immediately charged downstream, a loop of fly line caught on my reel, and the leader instantly popped.

Jim remained silent, as good fishing partners will during moments of crushing defeat. He readied the canoe as I reeled the slack line up through the guides of my rod and into the reel. I was done fishing, at least for the afternoon. A minute later I hauled myself into the boat, dropped my rod in the bilge, and began paddling.

By the time we reached the campsite, the spell had broken. Birds once again chattered away: wood thrushes, Canada warblers, veeries, each song prettier than the last. An otherwise perfect day on the upper Delaware continued on, minus one fisherman and one very large rising trout. *(August 24, 2003)*

GETTING COLD AND WET PROVES
WORTH THE EFFORT

By Peter Kaminsky

THERE IS A disquieting inevitability to that split second between the moment you know you have stepped too far into a swift current and the moment it overflows your waders. You have a clear sense of having reached the tipping point, a feeling of the world slowing down as it does before a traffic crash. There is nothing you can do about it except get wet.

Recalling the experience now, as the bleak days of winter keep all but the most intrepid anglers inside, it takes on the tone of a shaggy-dog tale:

The adventure started when we drove down an old logging road to the wildest stretch of the West Branch of the Ausable in the Adirondacks. My companions were my longtime fishing partner, Tom Akstens of Bakers Mills, New York, and Fritz Mitchell of Charlotte, Vermont.

When we arrived at the river, the air was wet with a passing rain. The understory of the forest was a thicket of aspen, wildflowers, and pale green caribou moss. The leaves dripped with heavy summer mist, and mosquitoes feasted on all warm-blooded creatures. In the late golden sun, the flutter of insect wings filled the air with sparkling light. *Isonychia,* large gray mayflies, hatched in numbers.

Even larger *Isonychia* spinners dipped to the surface of the river; because of their long white legs they are known as White Gloved Howdies (so called after old politicians who wore white gloves on their glad-handing forays).

The water was high. The wading was a bear. Fritz, who prefers to fish rough pocket water, spotted the broad shoulders of a rising fish. He directed me to the best place to cast across the complex current. I leaned on my wading staff and fought my way out. I cast. The fish rose. My fly dragged. The fish went down. I presented my fly again. The fish rose again, but, on subsequent casts, neglected to reappear.

"Funny thing, Fritz," I said. "My experience on pocket water is that the fish are opportunist and not too picky. They should keep rising to the fly."

"They will rise at first," he replied. "But I find that you get one or two shots and if they don't take, move on."

With that he suggested we move to the next good trout lie upstream. I turned in the current and inched toward shore. The river nudged me downstream. When I lifted my foot, it was like stepping off a ledge. As I tried to catch a foothold, I knew what was coming. I didn't have enough purchase on the bottom to move backward. I had to move forward at all costs. I tippy-toed until I was on point like a ballerina and then ran out of toe room. The water lapped over the top of my waders. Cold wetness filled my boots.

"At least you weren't swept downstream," Tom said.

Wet, but determined to get even with the trout, I joined my comrades for the march upstream. We forded at a nonsuicidal spot and entered the water below the outlet of a feeder creek. I waded gingerly into the flat water where I expected to see risers to the *Isonychia*. There were none.

Fritz waded into the pocket water with the ease of a bison walking through tall grass. He tied on a Gray Wulff and — bam, bam, bam, bam — took four nice brook trout. He advised me to cast near some rocks and to pass by others. Every rock that he thought would yield a trout, did: all lovely brookies.

"If you are up for it," he said, "the flat rock below the pool takes some wading, but I know there's a nice fish there."

"No way," I said, faintheartedly.

"You're doing it," he said.

I fought through the current, bird-dogging Fritz's footsteps. He found a spot where there was enough gravel to dig in. He gave me a Stimulator, a good pocket-water pattern that imitates a large stonefly. Per his instructions, I laid out a long cast and threw an upstream mend when it hit the water. The fly floated through a slick and then past the trunk of a deadfall against the far bank.

Nothing.

I cast again. The fly spun in the eddy. Just at the point where the line was going to begin to drag, a large, fat rainbow slammed it and in the same motion launched itself a foot into the air.

Tom whooped with excitement. Fritz, too. He counseled me to edge backward to the bank and then to fight the fish as I followed downstream. I declined: I would beat the fish where I stood or I would lose him, but I was not going to take another dunking.

The rainbow proved pugnacious but compliant. Within minutes, I had him in my hands. He was the best fish and certainly the most dramatic one of my trip. Being cold and wet was, at that moment, very beside the point. *(January 14, 2001)*

DRAWN TO A WILD, REMOTE RIVER

By Nelson Bryant

U PTON, ME. — The Rapid River in Maine is only one of many places in northern New England to fish for landlocked salmon, but its relative inaccessibility — there are no public motor vehicle roads to it — and wild aspect tug at me anew each spring.

Tumbling northwest for about three miles from Pond in the River to Lake Umbagog, it is the swiftest-flowing river east of the Mississippi. Its growling, grinding roar makes it almost impossible to communicate with an angler less than thirty yards away on the opposite shore.

The river, as well as Pond in the River, holds landlocked salmon and brook trout, and only fly-fishing is allowed. No brook trout, a wild strain that includes fish in excess of three pounds, may be killed, and only one salmon — fourteen or more inches long — may be taken each day.

Lake Umbagog, which straddles the Maine–New Hampshire border, recently became a national wildlife refuge. There is a state park on its New Hampshire shore, and privately operated wilderness campsites are also available. I first visited the Rapid River by crossing Umbagog from the New Hampshire shore, and continue to do so. Others stay at Lakewood Camps on Lower Richardson Lake in Maine, and hike or mountain-bike to the Rapid River.

Ruth and I used to tent on Sunday Island, just off the Maine shore of upper Umbagog, but when we learned that there was a private camp at the mouth of the Rapid River that could be rented, we snapped it up. Owned by Dick and Liz Celli of Lenox, Massachusetts, it is closer to the fishing and has propane gas lights, a stove, a refrigerator, and a pitcher pump in the kitchen.

This year, as always, we went the first week in June, setting forth in our venerable twenty-foot Grumman canoe from the public launching site, a clearing in the woods on the south side of the Androscoggin River in Errol, New Hampshire, and motoring upriver three miles to Lake Umbagog. From that point, it is about a mile and a half to the Rapid River.

We leave our unwatched truck at the launching area for a week, and it has never been vandalized, not even the year I inadvertently left it unlocked, with the keys in the ignition. In years past we have paddled, but now a little two-horsepower outboard pushes our craft along at a good clip.

Save for a few deep holes, Umbagog is a long, shallow lake and exceedingly moody. Whitecaps and swells build up on it in a matter of minutes and can turn a crossing from a leisurely one-hour paddle into a strenuous and sometimes scary two-hour workout.

The Rapid River has several large salmon pools between Pond in the River and Umbagog, but I concentrate on its outlet pool, which is best fished by boat. I run the canoe up into the edge of the whitewater, anchor it from the bow, and make successive drops until I find fish.

Under outboard power, the camp we use is only fifteen minutes downriver, and we usually have the pool to ourselves from about 7:00 p.m. to dusk, because most of the other fishermen have to return to the other side of the lake. There are a half dozen other camps within a mile of ours, but they are rarely occupied in early June.

On our first evening at the outlet, while an eagle wheeled overhead and mergansers raced past, I caught and released one thirteen-inch salmon and lost another. The water was cold, 48 degrees, and I began to worry that it might remain so, thereby slowing the action. Ruth, who favors a sketch pad rather than a rod, was happy. The air temperature was in the fifties, and there were almost no blackflies or mosquitoes.

Save for two showery interludes, the following days were sunny but cool, with a northeast wind. Each day the water temperature rose, and by the time we left it was in the high fifties, and salmon were occasionally coming up for small mayflies that had begun to hatch. I caught legal-sized salmon, including two of nearly twenty inches, every day save the first, and my best outing was on the penultimate evening.

Then, with no other anglers about — save a pair of loons working a few yards from the canoe — I caught seven. All were taken on a sink-tip line with a standard Muddler Minnow, my favorite fly for the river's salmon at that time of year.

Returning to camp that evening, we found a yearling moose dining on alders beside the dock. He regarded us calmly, then stepped into the channel and swam across it to Hedgehog Island.

That night our meal was freeze-dried wild thyme turkey and rice. We expanded our salad with a few green cattail shoots that we had picked in a marsh upriver. We also varied our freeze-dried menu with grilled salmon, baked salmon with a chopped almond and butter sauce, and boiled crayfish.

The last evening, I decided to leave the salmon alone. I anchored the canoe on the edge of the drowned river channel in front of the camp and, using a Maynard Marvel fly, caught three smallmouth bass of more than two pounds each. I was entitled to keep one of them, but released them all. That little gesture of self-denial made our freeze-dried Black Bart Chili supper — eaten on the bug-free porch with the sun setting over the smooth, pollen-streaked lake as loons began their lament — more palatable than I had anticipated. *(July 13, 1997)*

ALIENS IN THE DELAWARE

ARE WELCOME TO STAY

BY PETE BODO

EPOSIT, N.Y. — The angler staggering up the steep bank to the hardtop road where Richard Franklin and I were stringing up our fly rods appeared dazed and contented, proving once again that people who grouse about "too much of a good thing" probably never experience it. This lean gent had caught so many trout that he regarded even the dense poison ivy carpeting the bank with delight: Oh, the waxy sheen of those leaves! Oh, that subtle crimson tint on the triple-leaf clusters!

"The Baetis were hatching heavy all morning," he said breathlessly, referring to a small mayfly commonly called the Blue Winged Olive. "There were Sulfur spinners, too, and some caddis. Every fish in the river was up, feeding." He allowed the requisite beat before the punchline: "They turned off about an hour ago. Must be this wind."

Undaunted, my partner and I soon scrambled down the footpath to the West Branch of the Delaware River. It was 3:00 p.m. on a sunny day in early June, a time we frequently fish in this area, just a few miles below the Cannonsville Reservoir. The river is braided up here, the islands dense with flowering briars, bleached-out deadfalls, and the detritus of the spring floods, which invariably includes a pair of navy blue New York Giants sweatpants grotesquely twisted around a willow root.

I find the flotsam intriguing, in a morbid way, but these islands are valuable as well as compelling. Inundated all spring, they explode with life as soon as the floods recede, and quickly become so dense that bushwhacking across even the most slender of them in waders is impossible. While it's inconvenient negotiating around them, they provide quality habitat for nesting birds and secure bedding areas for deer.

Islands also multiply the amount of bank habitat for trout and add to the available amount of food, provided the volume of water is sufficient to push up against them. Thanks to a wet spring, the West Branch was flowing at a robust 1,200 cubic feet a second, almost double the norm.

When a river is bank-full, its foliated banks provide juvenile trout with places to hide, adult trout with ideal feeding stations, and freshly hatched aquatic insects with good cover in which they rapidly mature before mating and sowing their eggs back into the river from which they sprang. Trout often take up bankside lies along islands for the same reasons that dogs like to feign sleep beneath dining-room tables: just in case something falls off the edge.

It took some looking, but Richard and I found fish rising sporadically in the broad back channel of the river. In a typical June, this flat would be glassy and the trout hard to fool. But the current was brisk and the surface simmered, tilting the odds our way. Reflections of purple and white dame's rocket shimmered in the late-afternoon light, and then a fish rose within casting range, completing the tableau.

As soon as my size-16 Parachute Adams alighted on the surface, the trout grabbed it. It was a fat, foot-long brown that burped at me as I slipped the barbless hook from its jaw. Strictly speaking, dame's rocket (a member of the mustard family, it closely resembles phlox) and brown trout are both aliens in the local ecosystem, but as far as I'm concerned they are more than welcome to stay. Just minutes later, Richard hooked and landed a considerably larger fish. Our reverie was interrupted by a thunderstorm. We scowled at the sky, huddling in our flimsy rain jackets.

Clearing, the skies were clotted with orange. It was so still that droplets fell audibly from the leaves. The broad channel before me was the color of pewter, open and inviting. But I kept casting glances over my shoulder at the island, expecting fish to rise there as dusk approached. They would be tight to the bank, in the dark band of water below the dank overhanging boughs that tippled the surface here and there.

Sulfurs, tiny yellow mayflies, began emerging in the failing light. Here and there, a snout poked through the surface. Trout in bank lies, where the current is usually slow and even, rise deliberately. Often their dorsal fins wag in the surface film. If you don't have a seizure at the sight, you can accurately judge the size of the fish.

None of the fish up against the island were giants. But in that microenvironment, even the little dumb ones can be challenging. Presenting a fly accurately, delicately, and realistically to a bank feeder is, to many anglers, the height of the art.

I patiently worked on the largest of the fish for half an hour. Just before dark, I finally hooked it on a size-18 Sulfur Emerger. I don't know which of us was more surprised. By the time I released the lovely fifteen-inch brown, it was dark. The chill air was heavy with the scent of alluvial earth. I'd have to wade around the edge of the entire island in the dark to get back to the car, and that was just fine by me. *(June 18, 2000)*

OF FALLEN FRUIT AND
FANCIFUL FISHING

By Nelson Bryant

ENTWORTH LOCATION, N.H. — Being an enthusiastic forager, I pulled my pickup truck off the
logging road that leads to Dartmouth College's Second
College Grant, a forty-two-square-mile chunk of wilderness in
northeastern New Hampshire, and I spotted a tree laden with
yellow apples standing alone in a forest clearing.

My companion, Ruth Kirchmeier, and I were headed for
several days of September solitude in the Grant's Hellgate
Gorge cabin on the Dead Diamond River. Among our provi-
sions were several packets of freeze-dried applesauce, but the
occasional apple trees — probably the result of seeds dropped
by birds a half century or more ago — along the eleven-mile
road to the gorge yield an assertive and delicious fruit that
cannot be matched by the produce of a coddled orchard.

Ruth and I discovered that nearly all of the fallen fruit
had been eaten by deer, bear, or moose, but I reminded her
that several miles ahead, near the bridge over Washburn
Brook, there was a much larger tree that usually bore heavily.
Not a single apple was aloft on the Washburn Brook tree, and
very few were on the ground. The tall wild grasses under the
tree had been beaten flat in places by the aforementioned crit-
ters, and the acrobatic bears had apparently climbed the tree
to get at the fruit.

This was confirmed by Lorraine Turner, the Grant's care-taker, who said that she had been photographing bear cubs on high in an apple tree. Knowing that Wentworth Location is a bit far north for successful growing of tomatoes, I had brought a basket of them from my own garden for Lorraine. When she returned the basket a few days later, it was filled with wild apples.

The usual reasons for my trips to the Grant — not forgetting a sometimes frantic urge to escape the press of my own species — are to hunt ruffed grouse or deer or to fish the Dead Diamond or its major tributary, the Swift Diamond, for trout. The Dead Diamond watershed is one of the few places west of Maine to harbor wild brook trout, and the fish have been barely holding their own for decades. There are various reasons for this, including overfishing, intensive logging in years past, and warming air and water temperatures. Dartmouth owns most of the watershed. In recent years it has instituted enlightened logging practices, and it has set aside three large natural areas not to be cut except when the trees are killed by disease. The college asks anglers to keep no more than two trout daily, and suggests that releasing all of them would be even better.

Trout fishing was once superb on the Dead Diamond. In a column in the spring in the *Concord* (New Hampshire) *Monitor,* William Lange quoted an 1889 account of angling in the Hell-gate area: "An hour's float down the river any evening just at sunset will fill a ten-pound basket with fish from one-quarter to one pound in weight."

I fly-fished the pool just above the gorge and caught a couple of small trout, which I released. Early that evening I saw a big trout — certainly well over a pound — rise to take an insect from the deep, dark water near the head of the steep-sided gorge. It rose repeatedly for half an hour, but was in a spot that could not be covered by a shore-based fly-fisherman.

Lorraine lent me her float tube. With it I managed to reach a spot from which I could cast to the trout's lair. My passage up the current resembled that of a half-drowned grasshopper. From four o'clock to sunset, I sat on a big boulder that was pockmarked with holes scoured out by swirling stones and high water over centuries, periodically drifting various dry flies over the chosen location. I was certain that persistence would be rewarded, but I never saw that trout again.

The following day, Ruth and I hiked to Hellgate Pond, a three-acre trout pond about a mile up a forested hillside southwest of Hellgate Gorge. It proved unfishable with what was needed — a sinking line — because of a vigorous bloom of water lilies and sago pond weed. My fly was festooned with vegetation on almost every cast.

Two days later we left the solitude of the Grant, went a few miles south to Errol, New Hampshire, and launched our canoe in the big pool directly below the hydroelectric dam on the Androscoggin River. My second cast with my version of a Maynard Marvel streamer fly resulted in a savage strike from a big fish, probably a landlocked salmon. I had no more hits with that fly, so I switched to a dry, a Royal Wulff. Several small salmon vaulted out of the water in pursuit of it, but none were hooked.

The following afternoon we visited a lovely run on the Androscoggin several miles south of Errol. I donned waders and, with the aid of my wading staff, positioned myself in midstream, holding back on casting until a happy group of chattering, river-running canoeists had passed. The Androscoggin and its more sedate tributary, the Magalloway, are heavily used by canoeists and kayakers.

Late in the day, when the low-slanting sun was touching reddening maples on the distant hills with a holy light, both trout and landlocked salmon began to come up for emerging aquatic insects. In the forty-five minutes that this went on, I caught — all except one on dry flies — one salmon, three brook trout, and one brown trout, returning them all to the river, with thanks to the gods of the chase.

I would have kept the salmon if it had not been just below the fifteen-inch minimum length limit. In our grub box were three little jars — wasabi mustard, pickled ginger, and soy sauce — with which I would have created a celebratory salmon sashimi. *(October 5, 2003)*

MANHATTAN AS A PARADISE FOR
TROUT AND FLY-FISHING

By Nicholas Karas

COLONISTS ON MANHATTAN took their brook trout seriously. So seriously that they insisted that their fishing be protected from commercial exploitation. On May 28, 1734, New York City's Common Council passed a law restricting brook trout in "Freshwater Pond" to those who fished for fun and food. The law was written to forbid the use of nets, engines, or other devices to take fish in the pond, "other than by angling, with angle-rod, hook and line only."

The law was unique when compared with earlier laws passed elsewhere. It did not deal with seasons or limits, but only with the manner in which fish could be taken. The pond and its outlet stream had been a fishing ground since French fur traders established a temporary village on its shores in 1540, next to the bark houses of the Warpoes Indian band.

This may seem a little heady — Manhattan as a reserve for brook trout — to be grasped by anyone familiar with the city. It is impossible for most people to comprehend, let alone believe, that this Isle of Joy is where sportfishing began. Manhattan once was a sportsman's paradise. Its ponds, lakes, and freshwater streams were glutted with brook trout.

Its most famous pond was not the Pond — a shallow, man-made skating rink in Central Park — but Collect Pond, in Lower

Manhattan. Also known by colonists as Freshwater Pond, it was a quarter-mile long (between what are now Duane and Canal Streets), an eighth of a mile wide (between Lafayette and Mulberry Streets), and sixty feet deep.

In almost a straight line on a west-northwest heading, Ishpetenga, one of the largest streams on Manhattan, drained the overflow of Collect Pond into North (Hudson) River, a half-mile away. During the seventeenth and eighteenth centuries the stream and pond provided residents of Lower Manhattan with a constant supply of fresh water and fish.

It took the English, however, during their occupation of Manhattan while the Revolutionary War was being fought, to make Americans appreciate recreational fishing. Many of the British officers were tutored in fly-fishing. Recreational angling had been in vogue for more than one hundred years after Izaak Walton's *Compleat Angler* was published in Britain in 1653.

Americans watched in awe as the English, with their fine rods and delicate flies, fished the island's ponds and trout streams. But even in England, only the gentry had enough leisure time to pursue fishing for fun. In colonial America, an affluent merchant class was only in the initial throes of formation. They learned quickly, however; after the English were evicted, Manhattan became the seat of sportfishing for a few decades.

During the late 1700s, one of the most popular fishing pools on the Ishpetenga was at the base of the Stone Bridge, where Broadway crossed the stream at Canal Street. Collect Pond (there was also a Little Collect Pond that drained into the bigger body of water) was abandoned as a source of drinking water because of pollution, and filled in by 1803. Fill came from nearby hills on Broadway and Chatham Square, and brook trout were no more.

To drain the pond, the outlet creek had to be made deeper, and it became known as the Canal. For a while after the pond was filled, brook trout continued to spawn and live in the Canal. The creek's lower portion, near the Hudson River, had a short tidal section that produced salters, sea-run brook trout. It had long been the colonial angler's favorite spot.

Today, Collect Pond, with its creeks and canal, exists only in history books and on a street sign. Federal Plaza, Foley Square, and the City Prison (the Tombs) sit on the site. Only during protracted periods of heavy rain does the pond try to reemerge as storm drains overflow into the streets and water seeks to find the North River.

❧   ❧   ❧

There's one monument to the Collect's brook trout. Unknowingly, a former Wisconsin restaurateur and devotee of brook trout created the Anglers & Writers Restaurant at 420 Hudson Street. Next door he opened an antique shop, the Bespeckled Trout, a shrine to brook trout.

Though the Ishpetenga and the Collect were popular with trout fishermen, they were not the only brook trout waters on Manhattan. The island's transformation from a forested islet to a bucolic countryside, then a suburban and finally urban monolith, took place rapidly between the early 1700s and 1800s.

The first fish to disappear were the demanding brook trout as their habitat was dried up, filled, or turned into natural sewage conduits.

Manhattan anglers, however, did not feel hindered by the loss of trout-fishing opportunities immediately adjacent to where they lived. After all, Long Island was just a short ferry ride to the east, and its brook trout streams were boundless. *(February 22, 1998)*

A TROUT TRYST: WAITING
FOR YOU IS THE BIG ONE

BY PATRICIA LEIGH BROWN

EVERY ONCE IN a while, when the religion and incense hawkers around Times Square become too much and the unmuffled scent of New York City shish kebab threatens to cling to the clothes forever, I do what so many other urban anglers do. I flee. I head out to a dream of a stream, to a place in Suffolk County, Long Island, that is filled with gentle forest creatures, a bewitching green refuge that feels like a scene out of *Bambi* (if you ignore the ticks).

Anglers, not unlike criminals, tend to return to the place where they've caught fish. For me, that place is (usually) the Connetquot River State Park Preserve in Oakdale, a crystalline, spring-fed stream less than an hour and a half's drive from the city.

Well, let's be honest. I don't always catch fish. As a Mother's Day present, my husband drove me to the Connetquot recently so that I could have a few blissful hours to myself on the stream. It had been a year and a half since I'd done any fly-fishing. With raindrops pelting down, making thousands of little dimples on the water, it was difficult to see any trout rising. The temperature was numbing, the casts wobbly. The pathetic sight of a new working mother desperately flailing the water with stiff fingers in her three hours of free time resembled Lucy Ricardo in the chocolate factory, not Bambi.

But there have been other days, glorious days. Spring days, when the river's rush and the splash of a muskrat's tail were the only sounds, and the cool, clear water of the Connetquot (pronounced kuh-NET-kwat, a Wingan-Hauppaug Indian term for "wide" or "great" river) flowed into the spirit like a life-force.

The experience of fishing the Connetquot (fly-fishing only, with barbless hooks) really begins at the parking lot. It is the cement-paved gathering of the brethren, whose raised car trunks reveal waders, fishing rods, and stream thermometers. To do any fly-fishing at the Connetquot, which operates on the British "beat" system by reservation only, it is necessary to book one week in advance. The more fanatical anglers may be spotted the night before February 1 — the official opening day here — sleeping in their cars overnight for the privilege of fishing at the crack of dawn.

In the parking lot, the latest intelligence is exchanged on stream conditions and what kind of lures the fish seem to be taking that day. But not too much intelligence. One reason fishing vests seem to contain so many pockets is that they are loaded with secrets, locked in Velcro.

It is about a mile's hike from the parking lot to the stream, and, despite the unwieldiness of walking in waders, it's like walking into a little bit of heaven. The welcoming committee includes wild turkeys, peacocks, and deer. The preserve contains about two hundred species of birds, and a delicate ecosystem that captures some of the way Long Island used to be, before the Long Island Expressway, octoplexes, and IKEA. The water is cool and clear, perfect for trout. The spring-fed stream percolates through sand and gravel — sand being one of nature's most efficient filters, a cosmic Melitta.

Dreaming of trout, I walked past rambling old cedar-shingle clubhouses, their windowsills painted a deep forest green. Some of these buildings, including an old gristmill on the river, were erected by the South-Side Sportsmen's Club of Long Island, an "assembly of good fellows" who purchased the property in 1865.

What is now known simply as "the Connetquot" was the site of Snedecor's Tavern, a stagecoach stop built by Eliphalet Snedecor, known as Eli, a farmer. Snedecor's was the watering hole of choice for what is now the town of Islip, within shooting distance (literally) of choice hunting and fishing grounds.

In 1865 a group of sportsmen who were having trouble booking rooms at the inn decided to purchase it and the 300-acre family farm for $42,000 from Obadiah Snedecor, known as Obie, Eli's son. The South-Side Club was a place for monied gentlemen bearing names like Bayard and Bradish to meet, fish, and shoot.

Its members included many illustrious sportsmen, including Ulysses S. Grant and Charles L. Tiffany, the jeweler. According to Richard P. Baldwin, a Patchogue historian, on November 12, 1842, John Delmonico, the famed New York City restaurateur, supposedly died of apoplexy at the edge of the stream. It was rumored he had died of "buck" or "deer" fever, an affliction of hunters overly excited by the sight of game.

I have an inkling of what buck fever was like. Standing in the water, seeing a lone shadow suddenly lurching — a trout! — I understand apoplexy. Despite X-rays, vaccinations, and other medical miracles, I know for a fact that a girl can die of trout fever.

Among anglers, the Connetquot is known to harbor some really big fish. You can see them (unfortunately, they can see you). Part of the reason there are so many big fish here is that the preserve, now 3,400 acres, which was designated in 1987 as the first state park preserve in New York, contains a fish hatchery owned and administered by the state and the Long Island State Park and Recreation Commission. Every year, says Gilbert Bergen, the park manager, about 300,000 brook trout eggs, 280,000 rainbow trout eggs, and between 280,000 and 300,000 brown trout eggs are raised, about a quarter of them to adult size, up to three pounds or more.

Like parents learning Lamaze, Mr. Bergen and his crew are unusual in their commitment to rearing the trout as "naturally" as possible, using the river's own flow to nurture them. Once or twice a week they release them, nine- to twelve-inch yearlings up to two- to three-pound oldsters. Although there is no proof, the prevailing theory is that some of these larger trout make their way through the river to the saltwater of the Great South Bay and then return. The evidence, Mr. Bergen says, is that the fish come back bright and rich and silvery, as if they've just come back from trout Acapulco.

My favorite place to fish is a specific stretch — I won't divulge its location — a long, shallow run of water where delicate water star-worts, cresslike plants, decorate the underwater landscape like a wreath.

The Connetquot does not possess the weighty history of the Beaverkill and some other fabled regional angling spots (oh, lack of storied anglers — what a liberating thing you are!). But it does possess the beat system. The beat system, in which a certain spot on the river is reserved for a certain angler, is a holdover from European feudalism, according to the angling historian Ernest Schwiebert. Fishing rights were part of property rights, the fish in private waters part of the King's game.

At Connetquot, though, the beat system is a bastion of democracy. It enables the angler to reserve his or her own spot on a first-come-first-served basis. All access to the preserve, be it for hiking or fishing, is by reservation only. It is a means of environmental conservation, protecting the park and the trout from being overrun, otherwise known as opening-day-on-the-Beaverkill syndrome. For a novice, the privacy is a godsend: you can make ridiculous casts into hard-fighting bushes and nobody will see you do it.

On that woeful rainy Mother's Day, even the faint whiff of skunk after a long winter in the city was restorative. "Have you tried a Woolly Bugger?" said an acquaintance, taking pity on my failures and trying to be helpful.

So I tried the Woolly Buggers, long black feathery streamers. They did yield about ten hits, all of which I managed to miss. The trout began to feel like errant children. "Happy Mother's Day, sucker," they bubbled. "Nyah, nyah, nyah, nyah, nyah."

My acquaintance, a seasoned angler, sensed my frustration and was moved to charity. Having caught and kept two monstrous trout in his first hour of fishing, he offered to give them to me (for him there were more where they came from; the same could not be said for me). These trout were so big that when I put them in my creel, they thrashed so hard that the creel started bouncing down the trail.

I put aside my pride (it was Mother's Day, after all) and accepted his noble offer. For the next week we dined like kings, trout on the grill, our spirits spring-fed like the stream. *(June 7, 1992)*

TRUMPING RULES OF A
PRIVATE PARADISE

By John van Vliet

N OT LONG AGO I had the opportunity to fish a stretch of trout stream that doesn't see a lot of pressure — private water, to be precise. This particular river runs much of its course through a ranch owned by a celebrity who uses the 45,000-acre spread as a retreat. And while I've always had a nagging moral problem with private water, I'm not against having fun. So, when a friend of mine who owns a fly shop in Montana invited me to join him on a stream very few anglers get permission to fish, naturally I jumped at the chance.

I was out west working on a new book, but with a little too much emphasis on working and not enough on fly-fishing. I'd been living in a tiny log cabin in West Yellowstone for nearly a month. The work was fine, but the days were long, hot, and dusty. I was hungry for the chance to relax, cast a fly to a few uneducated trout away from the heavily fished streams around Yellowstone.

The day before we were to fish, the fly-shop owner told me he had called up to the ranch and cleared everything with the owners, who he admitted could be a little "funny" about strangers.

The next morning broke clear and hot with the promise of a stiff breeze by midday. I packed my gear in the truck, including a cooler full of good locally brewed beer and sandwich fixings for the two of us, and I drove the short distance to the fly shop. But business had come up and my friend could not go. So he drew a map on his business card.

It was adequate, though decidedly not to scale, and although I didn't get lost, the unpaved part of the trip took much longer than I'd planned. The sun was already high when I passed through an unmarked gate and parked the truck in front of the caretaker's cabin another quarter mile down the two-track ranch road.

The river was a classic Montana freestone stream tumbling out of the nearby mountain range and gathering clear, cold water from countless small tributaries, feeder seeps, and springs along the way. At this point in its journey, the stream was still losing altitude fast, making for sections of swift pocket water broken by occasional deep runs and pools. It flowed just a few steps from the caretaker's cabin and divided the ranch from the rest of the world like a moat, spanned only by a single narrow wooden bridge.

I walked around the front of the truck and up the steps of the caretaker's house and knocked at the sun-bleached door. As I waited for an answer, I heard a soft hissing just audible above the voice of the river. I looked back at the truck and noticed a small plume of steam erupting from the slowly deflating right rear tire. I also saw immediately that I'd parked the truck on a fairly steep little slope leading down to the bridge, making it virtually impossible to put up a jack safely.

Without waiting for an answer at the door, I jumped into the truck and drove across the bridge to a level spot just below the main house. I opened the overloaded tailgate and rooted around until I found the jack. I retrieved the jack handle from under the hood and began wrestling the spare from its roost.

That's when a deep voice behind me asked just what I thought I was doing.

The voice belonged to a large — but, mercifully, unarmed — ranch hand named Dave, who softened up when I mentioned the fly-shop owner's name. Seems the shop owner's idea of "clearing it" with the landowner was to leave a message on the caretaker's answering machine, which, naturally, everyone was too busy to check. As a result I wasn't exactly expected. And no one seemed remotely thrilled that I was there.

By the time we'd gotten things cleared up, several other ranch hands had appeared along with the landowner's wife, who rode up on horseback. She knew vaguely who I was and invited me to stay — provided I agree to three conditions: 1. No photographs of the place. 2. Return all fish to the stream. 3. Never, ever tell anyone I'd been there. This last part she said with as polite and sweet an or-I'll-turn-my-boys-here-loose-on-you as I'd ever heard. I agreed, of course, and went back to the business of changing my tire.

By now the sun was directly overhead, and a breeze had kicked up, stirring the dry corral into small columns of dust that swirled around me as the temperature edged toward 90. And I was no closer to fishing than I'd been all day.

I offered Dave and the other boys a beer and jacked up the truck. I changed the tire as the boys sat on a fence and drank their beers. They got into a discussion of their respective high school football injuries and took turns climbing into the teetering three-wheeled truck to pluck another beer out of my cooler.

I did eventually fish the stream. I had the water to myself, the fish were easy to fool, and I forgot all about the work I'd left behind. So I guess it worked out pretty much the way I'd hoped. But I couldn't get away from the nagging feeling that this stream was no different from any other stream I'd fished out there, with one exception: the seventy square miles surrounding it belonged to a guy who lived in New York City.

I felt like Cinderella, invited to a swanky ball for just one night but all the while waltzing with one ear cocked for the tolling of the clock. Private water just ran contrary to my sense of what's fair, although I knew if I owned a nice piece of water, I might hold a different opinion. But for the time being, I decided to stick to the public waters and take my chances of running into other folks like me: ordinary people who work to live and live to fish.

Just before I was going to call it quits for the day, as the sun sank toward the mountains and the breeze began to die, I hooked a nice fish on a Jacklin's Hopper I'd slapped under the overhanging branches of a small streamside willow. The trout fought wildly, and when I landed it, I saw the seventeen-inch rainbow had taken the hopper deep and torn itself up. It was clear it wasn't going to survive, with blood in its gills and the fierce fiery color fading from its eyes. I weighed the consequences and decided to keep the fish for my dinner, out of respect.

I didn't feel good about it, but I'd released all the other fish I'd caught, and I knew it was the right thing to do. You'd have done the same. It didn't seem appropriate to continue fishing, so I started back to my truck. At the crest of a high ridge overlooking the stream, I paused to admire the way the low red sun was painting long blue shadows across the sage-green valley and the cluster of buildings that made up the ranch. I stopped just long enough to snap a single photograph and moved on.

Sure, I remembered what the landowner's wife had said and the three rules to which I'd agreed under duress, but I wasn't going to release a dying fish and I couldn't pass up a nice photograph. After all, I rationalized, it wasn't like I was stealing. These wealthy celebrities had a nice ranch, money in the bank, and privacy of which the rest of us can only dream. Nothing I did was going to take that away from them — unless perhaps I broke the third rule. *(February 2, 2003)*

TAPPING PLUMP BROWNS,

WITH A BAYOU NYMPH

By Adam Clymer

TROUT FOR BREAKFAST has fallen out of favor in recent years, except at posh hotels like the Brown Palace in Denver, where the cornmeal-crusted rainbow is still a menu highlight.

Most of the time I fish in places like Montana, where killing fish is greedy because the state has abandoned stocking to promote its wild populations, or I fish strange streams with guides who insist on releasing the fish to keep their home waters productive.

Keeping an occasional stocked fish (knowing that many local anglers keep several) hardly seems sinful. And it has been years since I have been to the Brown Palace. So the plump, nine-inch brown, a stocked fish with fins worn from growing up in a concrete pen, was too tempting to release after it took a small elk-hair caddis near dusk in early May on Duschee (pronounced Dutchy) Creek in Minnesota near Lanesboro.

John van Vliet, who had organized the trip, took one that evening, too, and together with eggs and bacon they made a delicious, tender breakfast for us, my wife, Ann, and Greg Farley, who showed the cook at Lanesboro's Chat and Chew just how the trout should be fried in butter.

Duschee is a spring creek that carves its way around lime-stone hills of what is known as the driftless region because there is no glacial drift left behind from the last glacial age, which began about two million years ago and lasted until the ice nearby began melting about 18,000 years ago.

Thomas F. Waters, a retired professor of fisheries at the University of Minnesota's St. Paul campus, said the glaciers missed this area because it was a plateau that they slid past. It covers about 16,000 square miles, mostly in Wisconsin but with a chunk of Minnesota and slivers of Iowa and Illinois.

Its rolling hills and steep valleys, carved out of sedimentary rocks from an earlier epoch when the land was beneath an ocean, produce rich farmland and a superb, alkaline trout habitat.

After Saturday's trout breakfast, we set off across the Mississippi River to Wisconsin and fished Timber Coulee near Coon Valley. We each got a few small fish, but there were always other fishermen in sight, so we drove another fifty miles to the implausibly named Big Green River near Fennimore. Ten to fifteen feet wide, it is all catch-and-release, so there was no one else fishing when we arrived and climbed over the ladderlike stiles that Wisconsin's Department of Natural Resources has erected over fences where it has fishing easements.

Neither John nor I did anything with dry flies, though we saw an occasional rise as the stream curved back and forth. But it was here that Greg came into his own, with a device he called the Bubba nymph because he had first seen it on the Chattahoochee River in Georgia.

The Bubba nymph, in John's phrase, "looks like a soft hackle on steroids." It is tied on a size-10 shiny steel jig-head hook — something that is more likely to be used for catching bream in the bayous. The eye for the leader hangs down toward the hook, causing the fly to drift upside down and avoid weeds. It has a green, yellow, or red microchenille body, a peacock-herl shoulder, and a collar of Hungarian partridge about the length of the hook, swept back.

Greg fished a deep pool up against a hillside and took several browns up to sixteen inches long on dead drifts. Then he gave me a couple of nymphs and climbed up the hill to smoke a cigar and watch the fishing from an angle where he could see the trout at the bottom of the pool.

I probably fished for thirty frustrating minutes. Occasionally I would get a light bump on the fly, and once one of those double tugs where a better angler would have set the hook. Greg kept telling me there were some big rainbows that would occasionally look at the nymph, and finally one took it and dashed down the pool and then back up. Greg clambered down the hill with his net, and the trout ran from it twice before he landed it—twenty-one inches and more than five pounds. The trout had almost straightened the hook in the fight.

Greg had relinquished the pool to me as a friendly gesture. I relinquished it out of necessity—to some black cows who sloshed through a few minutes later, apparently deeming the grass greener and tastier on my side of the water.

So that rainbow was the only trout I caught that day, though Greg took his Bubbas off to another stretch and caught several more browns.

I took one more breakfast-sized brown that Sunday morning, on a tiny Parachute Adams, but released it because we had already breakfasted and were on our way back to the Minneapolis–St. Paul airport. We detoured to another stream, called Trout Run, where Greg and John caught several more browns—all on the magical Bubba—and all three of us were soaked when the fine weather finally broke and an all-day rain began. *(June 23, 2003)*

FINDING A LITTLE PARADISE IN
FISHING THE TAILWATERS

By Peter Kaminsky

C RAIG, MONT. — As an angler, I cannot think of a more perfect town than this hamlet. It has two restaurants, one breakfast joint, two fly shops, and forty-two full-time residents. No newspaper, no museum, no professional sports team. Nothing but fly-rodders and trout.

The situation is rendered even more paradisiacal when the trout are cooperative, yet not recklessly compliant. Such foolhardiness is rarely the case with the well-fed trout of the Missouri River.

This tailwater fishery issues from the Holter Dam at Three Rivers and carries with it the waters of the Madison, Jefferson, and Gallatin Rivers. As a result, it is rich in nutrients and remains trout-pleasingly cool even in the blazing summer sun.

Some admirable traditionalists prefer the free-flowing Yellowstone or upper Madison, dismissing tailwaters as trout fishing's version of a silicone implant. But if casting to rising wild fish in calm water haunts your dreams as it does mine, then nothing surpasses this giant spring creek.

Our guide, Joe Cummings of A Classic Journey Outfitters, met my fishing partner, Josh Feigenbaum, and me for breakfast at 7:00 a.m. By that time, clouds of Trico spinners were

51

gyrating in the final hour of their mating dance. As the mayflies began to die, rising trout dimpled the water, feasting on the freshly fallen food.

Almost as thickly packed as the feeding fish, guides launched their drift boats into the flow.

"Let's head downriver so we can get ahead of the crowd and stake out a pod," Cummings said.

Within a half hour, Cummings had us on the water and in position in front of a rising pod. He took the measure of my cast and positioned me for a forty-foot left-reach cast.

I could barely restrain myself when he said, "I want you to see the fish first. There are a bunch of trout, but the best one is rising almost straight downstream."

I squinted through the slight glare, and I could see the pale form of the trout. It was holding in the current, finning, dropping down, turning, and floating up to sip a fly. The sight of the trout going about its life, unmindful of our presence, was supremely seductive.

In such circumstances, I think of coming upon a doe drinking at a quiet pool, or a wood nymph sitting on a moss-covered rock, combing her long hair. You hold your breath. You try not to move. You know that if your presence were known, the object of your desire would disappear.

Twenty casts later, the fish rose to my fly. I set the hook with slightly less grace than a 300-pound woodchopper wielding his ax. Feigenbaum and Cummings were sympathetic, if derisive.

Feigenbaum took his turn in the bow and shortly had hooked a nice fish. I was eager to return to the best position again, and when I did, I lost two or three more trout before hooking a two-pound rainbow — as fat as a pumpkin seed.

It ran like crazy, and with 5X tippet I knew I could apply some pressure, but not much. When I finally brought the fish to hand, Feigenbaum said, "Adding in all the fish you missed, it took an hour and a half for that baby. I knew you needed to catch a fish, so I sat and shut up."

I made a note to send him $10 million someday, when I have it on hand.

For the balance of the day, Cummings, who is powerfully built and indefatigable, kept drifting down on the same pod, then rowing back upstream for another pass. In this manner, we hooked a few more fish before continuing the float and switching to hopper imitations, which the fish really clobbered. We pulled off the water at 11:00 p.m., not realizing our fatigue until we laid down our rods.

❖   ❖   ❖

Back in town, Isaak's Café was hopping. The crowd bore the raccoon-face tan that results from days on the water looking through sunglasses. One guide pounded out country blues on an acoustic guitar, while the rest of the patrons kept time, sipped beer, devoured burgers, and relived trout caught, not yet caught, and still waiting to be caught.

The next morning the Tricos and the fish were at it again. Cummings made straight for the scene of the previous day's fishing. The trout were on the feed again, except they had dropped a bit downstream to quieter water. The cast had to be farther and the presentation even more delicate.

For whatever reason, I was as much on my game that morning as I had been off it the day before, landing a half dozen trout on size-20 Tricos on 6X. Though Cummings expressed dismay at the sparseness of the spinner fall, I think it might have worked in our favor. Had it been more bounteous, perhaps the trout might not have taken the fly as eagerly.

In any event, who dwells on the reasons for good luck? You simply savor such moments and store them for the days when you need reason to hope. *(September 5, 2004)*

WYOMING RIVERS
PRODUCE TROPHIES

BY GREG THOMAS

I F YOU WANT to catch wild trout without burning a pile of calories, Wyoming's Wind River Range, where granite peaks thrust 13,000 feet into the sky and its fish grow to massive proportions, is not the place to be.

The Wind River Range, which stretches 100 miles across western Wyoming's sage-covered expanse, is considered some of the most remote and beautiful terrain in North America. Pine trees and aspens cover the foothills until those granite monoliths take over. But most of its trout lakes rest in designated wilderness areas, five or more miles away from roads, attainable only via foot power or horsepower, the kind that doesn't come with a set of reins and spurs.

As I recently found, the Winds require a measure of dedication and a healthy dose of lung power to appreciate.

During a trek into any of the Wind River's two hundred or so lakes, anglers may be required to negotiate several thousand feet of elevation gain, accompanied by a forty-pound backpack and maybe a blister or two. Those who prefer their angling with a bottle of wine and a plate of cheese and crackers resting on the tailgate need not apply. But do keep in mind, remote lakes don't see much, if any, angling pressure, and the trout contained within them grow to large size. The Winds hold rainbow, brook, cutthroat, and golden trout, and all achieve or even exceed the magical twenty-inch mark, a length that separates a nice western trout from a true hog.

And the Wind Rivers remain one of the last bastions for golden trout, a fish so painted in pastel, a combination of subtle gold and orange, highlighted by a penetrating red slash, that they become almost impossible to describe accurately. Most people simply call goldens the most gorgeous of trout species. The largest goldens in the world swim in the Wind Rivers.

Golden trout originated in the Sierra Nevada Mountains of California, but they seldom exceed a pound in their native waters. Goldens were first introduced to the Wind River's barren lakes in the 1940s, carried in crates on the backs of horses and released in select waters. Those fish immediately took hold. Wyoming's current state-record golden, which was taken in the Wind Rivers at Cook Lake in 1948, weighed eleven pounds!

I was looking for the world-record golden—a fish weighing twelve to fifteen pounds—during my two-week, 100-mile trek through the Winds. I was armed with three fly rods, an assortment of sinking and floating fly lines, several hundred fly patterns, enough pasta to satisfy the most staunch Italian, and a professional photographer to record the historic catch.

We began our quest at the northern edge of the mountain range, covering nine miles of nasty trail to reach a lake high above timberline. I felt as if I were on top of the world, but my legs were incredibly shaky, my muscles twitching uncontrollably. Unfortunately, the lake held no goldens, although I did catch and release several nice cutthroats, including a seventeen-inch slab.

The following day we climbed four grueling miles to a lake once known to contain big goldens. I fished that lake, which rested at 11,200 feet, for several hours without sighting a fish, let alone garnering a strike. It was as if the Wind River lakes were barren once again and I was casting on a sea of futility. I fished several lakes in the area with the same result.

The following day, now on the eastern side of the range, we hiked eleven miles to a lake that a biologist had circled on my map. Along the trail we encountered two full-grown bull moose. We played a game of hide-and-seek with the largest bull, an 800-pound animal, as it wandered around a giant boulder, peeking at us as we peeked back.

When we reached our destination, exhausted and dripping perspiration, I was exalted. I could tell, just by looking at that gorgeous lake, with its deep center and shallow, fertile flats, that it contained big goldens. I held that notion through the first fifty strikeless casts. By one hundred casts I was discouraged and returned to our camp, which consisted of a tiny tent and a minuscule propane stove. That's when the lightning set in. Karen, the photographer, and I crouched under low vegetation for an hour or more as rain pelted our bodies and electric darts drilled the surrounding country.

The next day, having thrown at least five hundred casts, I gave up, declared the lake deserted, and told Karen to pack her bag.

As we exited the area, I spied a small lake tucked in a beautiful mountain bowl. We climbed down to the water and I immediately spotted a large trout finning near shore. I cast a beetle imitation near its position and the fish charged the fly, then struck as if it hadn't eaten in a week. I played the fish gingerly and finally landed the brute. It measured twenty-two inches long! Unfortunately the fish was a cutthroat, not a golden.

It was the kind of fishing that every fly angler dreams of — large trout that hold little regard for their safety contained in a beautiful setting, separated from the maddening pace of society by long miles of trail and a fresh mind-set.

Those anglers who know golden trout best are not surprised by my lack of success. They regard goldens as one of the most discerning, difficult trout species. They say goldens often feed solely on plankton, refusing flies as if they represented a plague.

Golden trout addicts say that late spring (which means late June and early July in the Wind Rivers), just as ice frees its grip on those mountain lakes, is the time to catch big goldens. Given good health and the will to carry backpacks through those rugged mountains, Karen and I will return to the Winds next year, determined to catch the world-record golden. We've contracted golden trout fever. *(December 24, 2000)*

OF GLEAMING TROUT AND

UNDYING FRIENDSHIP

By Nelson Bryant

Vic is dead and I am still trying to comprehend that unacceptable subtraction.

Vic Pomiecko and I met more than forty years ago when I became managing editor of the *Claremont* (New Hampshire) *Daily Eagle*, the newspaper in his hometown, and we began a lifetime of angling together, the first few decades focused on fly-fishing the region's remote trout ponds.

There are various trails to enduring friendships. Our route, born of a fierce urge to angle for the glorious squaretail trout in wild places, led through forests, alder swamps, and juniper thickets, past hillside homesteads abandoned a century before, to a lifetime of unspoken intimacy.

At one point we had sapling rafts — floated by four car-tire inner tubes and lashed together with nylon cord — on a dozen remote waters. We built the rafts on site and packed in the tubes and a pump on each trip. Some of the ponds were accessible by Jeep, but we couldn't afford top-quality fly rods, let alone a four-wheel-drive vehicle. Vic, a high school shop teacher, made us pack frames. I still have mine. He even fashioned himself a pair of hiking boots, and I thought he pushed frugality too far in this instance: rubber hip boots cut off at the ankle and held on with circlets cut from inner tubes.

We chose remote ponds because we had them to ourselves

most of the time. We became skilled at stillwater fly-fishing for trout, which can be as pleasurable — and as challenging — as flogging a stream.

Talk was sparse, particularly while we were fishing together. Even when we were standing six feet apart, balanced precariously on one of our rafts, half a day might pass with nothing more than an exclamation when a trout hit, or one asking the other what fly he was using. We were immersed in fishing and in shared solitude. Excessive talk would have intruded on the silence of the forest.

Later, sitting in the kitchen nursing our beers, words would come, but they were mainly a recapitulation of the day's adventure: of the trout and the flies they had favored, of the wild mushrooms we had gathered, of the grouse, deer, and beaver we had seen. Intimate feelings were revealed by indirection or default.

One winter, when barely a teenager, my youngest son, Jeff, wound up in the Claremont police station, beaten, drunk, and scared after his first encounter with booze. Vic went with me to fetch him. Jeff, who was slumped on a bench, whispered, "Take me home, Dad."

Stricken, but chary of showing emotion, I draped Jeff over my shoulder like a sack of grain, thanked the police, and departed. Vic, my wife learned from his wife, went home and wept. Although touched and surprised, I never mentioned his tears to him. It wasn't our style.

Usually quite taciturn, Vic would get excited when we burst out of the woods on the shore of a remote pond in October, our favorite time of year to fish, and trout were rising. Paying more attention to the rises than to what he was doing, he usually managed to miss a guide or two when stringing up his fly rod and would have to start all over again.

We fished on mornings so cold that we had to plunge our

rods into the water to melt the ice from the guides as mist curled from the pond and half-obscured the tattered yellow ensigns of shoreside birches.

On one such dawn at Cole Pond in Enfield, New Hampshire, Vic raised a giant brook trout — three to four pounds — that lifted from the depths of a cove near the outlet and made a pass at his streamer fly, then turned, red-gold flank gleaming, and descended.

"Quick!" Vic cried. "Cast to him!"

Telling me to try for a trophy trout that should have been his alone to woo was an offer of spontaneous generosity, and for me that fish — we never caught it — became a symbol of our friendship. It rises often and unexpectedly from the past, and thoughts of Vic rise with it.

For many years after I left Claremont for Martha's Vineyard, Vic and I visited our remote ponds in fall, but about a decade ago he had a small stroke and apparently decided — although he never said so — to limit himself to less strenuous excursions. He continued to fish readily accessible lakes and ponds near Claremont, and also visited me on the Vineyard to fly-fish for striped bass.

During his visits he reveled in retelling stories of our early days together. Within minutes I would join him. It was our way of celebrating our friendship without relinquishing reticence, a tribal chant, if you will.

Vic and another friend, John Houlihan, enjoyed a splendid evening of fly-fishing for bass on the Vineyard's Dogfish Bar with me last June. Vic died in his sleep several weeks later. Jeff, now in his mid-forties, was with us that night at Dogfish Bar, and a few days later he said that it had meant much to him to be able to give Vic tips on how and where to fly-fish for stripers at night, a tiny repayment for all the trout-fishing lore that Vic had shared with him.

Everywhere I turn, I am reminded of Vic.

There are the streamer flies — Royal Coachman bodies overlaid with gray squirrel tail — for brook trout, that I call Vic's Special, in one of my fly boxes. There is the dill flourishing in my garden; the seeds came from Vic. There are the tools in my workshop that were gifts from Vic: a wood lathe, a wonderful old hand-powered breast drill, an assortment of knives and chisels.

And while I am sentient, there will always be the great trout at Cole Pond rising from the deep and gleaming for an instant in the bright October sunlight. *(October 13, 1996)*

RETURNING TO THE PURE AND
SIMPLE JOYS OF FISHING

By Pete Bodo

ANDES, N.Y. — These days, walking any distance to go fishing is like leaping to pluck a gleaming apple off a bough and eating it on the spot. The scenario strikes a poignant, familiar chord in all of us. But few people actually do it. We buy our apples at the supermarket, and when we get a chance to fish, we drive right up to the roadside pullout beside the river and jump out, ready to go.

Thus, Richard Franklin and I decided that hiking in to fish for brook trout in a remote pond near this upstate community in the Catskills would be a novel way to end the trout season. Wild brookies, woefully sensitive and unspeakably lovely creatures, have gone the way of walking. These days, most fly-fishers want to match wits with tough, wily brown trout or zesty rainbows, neither of which is native to Northeastern waters. Moreover, we can drive our loaded sports utility vehicles within casting distance of them.

Meanwhile, the hapless native brookie is steadily pushed into the ever-diminishing nook of cold, pure water by its hardier and more flexible cousins, and by the degradation of the environment. We sometimes forget that a creature need not be fierce to be quintessentially wild.

An hour into our hike, bearing unwieldy inflated float tubes on our backs like gaudy blue-and-tan balloons, we were right back at square one. We had taken three wrong trails, and broken a sweat in doing so. We felt ashamed, with good reason. In his own way, each of us was thinking, "So it's come to this."

But we started off again, marching uphill, through stands of sturdy oak, cherry, beech, and ash trees. We hiked about two miles. Then, off in the distance below us, I saw through the blazing fall foliage the dark glint of water.

A twenty-pound porcupine, a creature with no reason to run even at the worst of times, allowed us to approach within about fifteen feet before it flared its neck and rump to display its ivory quills. It didn't even bother to turn head-on to confront us. The porcupine stood sideways, regarded us, and then waddled off along the shoreline.

Soon we had strapped on our flippers and plopped into the float tubes. These rigs, ingenious variations on the inner tube, allow anglers to maneuver and fish freely in still water of any depth. The trade-off is that you look like a floating bathtub toy, and feel as if you were nestled in a cushy Barcalounger. The only thing missing is the remote.

But the sensation is misleading, because these "belly boats" are quiet and unobtrusive, ideally suited for the low-impact approach that befits fishing in remote, pristine waters.

I called over to Richard. The ghastly echo of my voice startled me. By virtue of its surroundings, this pond demanded absolute silence. While neither of us had experienced that natural mandate in a long time, we grew accustomed to it quickly. And under that mantle of silence, wild brook trout tipped up their snouts and gently sipped tiny yellow mayflies from the surface of the black water.

Brookies are not discriminating feeders, nor are they spectacular fighters when stung by the hook. When it comes to that man-versus-fish thing, they just don't get it, any more than the great herds of bison understood the nature of the chase in the heyday of the great buffalo hunt. They just stood there and fell when shot. Likewise, brook trout will usually take any old fly, the gaudier the better, if you throw it in front of them. But even that is sometimes easier said than done.

The brookies of the pond were elusive, rising sporadically. By the time we cast to a rise, the fish were long gone. This was not the game of skill that fly-fishers crave to play with steadily rising trout. It was much more natural than that. Dead trees stood like giant bones at the marshy end of the pond, and behind them the colored hardwoods and handsome dark pines shivered in the light breeze and sparkled in the clear sunlight.

Eventually we paddled over to some odd structures barely visible on the far shore of the pond. It turned out that they were part of a spillway, slab concrete and steel pipe, man-made. But in the deep hole near the outflow we saw the fish — half a dozen of fifteen or sixteen inches, with broad olive backs. The conspicuous ivory edging on their fins identified them as brookies. The fish hung suspended in the water like paintings on a wall. Occasionally, one would leisurely swim a lap of the pool.

It was almost spawning time, and the big brookies probably gathered there because a hint of flow deceptively suggested the existence of a tributary in which they could find ideal spawning habitat. It didn't seem quite right to fish for them from atop a concrete culvert, but I did anyway. I didn't catch any. I guess at some level all of us were fooled, but I'm proud to say that we didn't get lost hiking back out to the car. *(October 4, 1998)*

SAVORING A SALMON

HOLDING POOL

By Nelson Bryant

L'ASCENSION DE PATAPEDIA, QUEBEC — Anchoring our canoe midway in the Patapedia Pool on the Restigouche River, my guide, Charles Irving, stood up, studied the water, and announced that there were a dozen salmon directly opposite us well within range of my fly rod.

I held off casting for a few minutes until I could make out the fish. This took a bit of doing because there were so many of them that I initially thought the clusters of dark shapes I saw resting on the light-colored bottom were rocks.

I stood, my rod in hand and all but forgotten, savoring the sight. It was my first visit to the Patapedia Pool, which is at the junction of the Restigouche and a tributary, the Patapedia. While I have gotten reasonably adept at spotting one, two, or three salmon lying in a stream, I had never before been treated to the sight of so many of them.

I was on the best salmon holding pool in the river. Fishing rights on the pool are owned by the Ristigouche Salmon Club — the club uses the ancient version of the spelling for *Restigouche*. According to Al Carter, who manages the club, the Patapedia Pool is "the best holding pool in North America," and few would disagree.

Terry and Jeanne Mathews of Nairobi, Kenya, and I were fishing as guests of Joseph Cullman III, a club member.

Cullman was also on the Patapedia Pool, and the Mathewses were about two miles downriver at the home pool of the club's Indian House lodge, where we were staying.

"Do you want to start with a dry fly or a wet fly?" Charles asked, apparently wondering if I was going to spend the remainder of the afternoon staring at the fish and marveling at their abundance.

I had rigged two rods and was holding the dry-fly outfit, so I began with it, striving to put my White Wulff fly in front of each fish in turn.

It was early August, and although the river was low and the water warm — far from ideal for salmon angling — I was filled with optimism generated by sheer numbers of salmon before me. Also, the wind had died and a fine rain was falling, conditions far superior to bright sunshine for salmon fishing. Surely, I thought, one of those would take a notion to seize my fly.

That notion was lurking in some of them. From time to time, salmon would come up from the bottom and slash at the fly or roll over it or bump it with their noses, but on none of those occasions were they pricked by the hook.

I had the feeling that the salmon were toying with me, but I didn't care. I was content to see them and raise them. Although I have caught most of my salmon on a wet, or sunken, fly, I prefer to fish with a dry. The sight of a salmon breaking the surface in quest of a floating fly snaps anglers to quivering attention, and if they are not properly disciplined they will often pull the fly away from the fish or wait too long and fail to set the hook.

This is a discipline about which much has been written, but it tends to elude explanation, as does a salmon's making a pass at your fly the first time it goes by, then ignoring it for thirty more casts, only to seize it fiercely on the thirty-first.

During the time that I was raising but not hooking salmon, Joe landed and released three.

❖   ❖   ❖

Darkness was close, and Joe and his guide, Brian Irving, departed. Charles, who had changed my dry fly several times, trying, among other things, two different sizes of one known as the Morris Killer, announced that we were running out of time and probably should switch to a wet fly.

On my third cast with a Rusty Rat, I hooked and kept a five-pound grilse, a salmon that returns to its natal stream after only one year at sea. In New Brunswick an angler may keep a grilse, but all multi-sea-year salmon must be released. (Quebec regulations allow an angler to take one salmon a day, but on the portion of the Restigouche that forms the boundary between the two provinces — from the river's mouth to the Patapedia junction — New Brunswick angling regulations apply.)

A few minutes later, a good salmon seized the same Rusty Rat. It was nearly defeated and within three feet of Charles's outstretched hand — he frequently tails a salmon with his hand rather than using a net — when the hook pulled free and the fish, which we estimated at fifteen pounds, swam away slowly into the deeper water.

I had played the fish properly, had enjoyed my ten-minute encounter with it, and was actually pleased that it had been able to release itself.

Back at Indian House, I learned that Terry had hooked and released a fifteen-pounder.

The following morning, Terry, Joe, and I were up early, savoring the view from the lodge, which is on a rise of land above the river. Occasional salmon and grilse were visible in the deep portion of the Home Pool before us. Later in the day, when the sun was high, we watched two schools of salmon of about forty fish each, circling slowly just below the surface.

On that same day, Charles allowed the canoe to drift over the slow, deep water in the lower end of the Patapedia Pool, and everywhere I looked there were salmon. Some were truly large, thirty pounds or more. In a few more weeks, as the days shortened and the nights grew cold, most of them would move upstream to spawn, some continuing on up the Restigouche, others ascending the Patapedia. In spring, dark and lean, those that survive will return to the Atlantic to feed and grow and recover the urge that will send them on another procreative odyssey. *(August 31, 1997)*

GOOD ALASKA FISHING

COMES WITH TIME

By Stephen Sautner

ACCORDING TO the *Book of Fishes* (National Geographic Society, 1952), a British surveyor investigating what is now British Columbia recommended that the region be left to the Americans because "the salmon will not rise to the fly." Obviously, he never fished with a Pink Pollywog.

Perhaps the world's ugliest salmon dry fly, the Pollywog is tied on a bass-bug hook with gobs of fuchsia marabou for a tail, followed by clumps of similarly colored deer hair spun and clipped to a potbellied shape. A finished one measures nearly four inches long and an inch wide. Comparing one to an artfully tied Jock Scott or Blue Charm would cause an Atlantic salmon fisherman to shudder in his tweeds.

But to silver (coho) salmon, the gregarious West Coast cousins of the Atlantic salmon, a Pollywog unceremoniously splattered down and chugged across a pool has the same effect as a home run ball hit into crowded bleachers at Yankee Stadium.

Or so I was led to believe by a fishing magazine I read a few years ago that guaranteed "a silver on every cast" with Pollywogs. This led to two trips to the heart of silver country in Alaska that ultimately proved disappointing, with me vainly casting Pollywogs to indifferent salmon, as indifferent fishing guides yawned behind me.

"Ever use a Pink Pollywog?" I would ask, grunting between double-hauls.

"No, but I heard they work," they would say in a tone reserved for clients with unreasonable requests. Yet not only did I fail to catch any salmon on Pollywogs, I also did poorly with more traditional fare such as Purple Egg-Sucking Leeches, Polar Shrimp, or Babine Specials.

So this year when I decided to head back to Alaska for one more shot at silvers, I decided to replace a fishing guide with something far more practical: a rented pickup truck. Then I chose Cordova, an isolated commercial fishing town in southwest Alaska, known for its glaciers, trumpeter swans, and the only known breeding area for dusky Canada geese. If I was going to be embarrassed or skunked again, I decided it would be in front of a few rare birds, or perhaps a wayward moose.

Cordova does have a handful of salmon rivers, some known only by their mile markers (Seven-Mile Creek, Eleven-Mile, etc.). Some run as clear as glass one year, only to clog with glacial silt the next, making reliable fishing here a risky proposition.

This year, however, silver salmon, not silt, clogged most of its streams, according to Matt Miller of the Alaska Department of Fish and Game, which operates a field office in downtown Cordova. "Right now, fishing is about as good as it gets," he said, quickly scribbling a map where a clearwater creek emptied into a tidal slough. Miller explained that with each high tide, new fish gathered, preparing to ascend the smaller streams to spawn.

An hour later I slogged through a wet field of sphagnum moss, armed with an 8-weight fly rod and a fly box filled with assorted silver salmon flies, including a generous supply of Pink Pollywogs.

Eventually I came to where the creek's tea-colored waters emerged from a tangle of alders and emptied into the slough. Low clouds promising rain hung over the snowcapped Chugach range in the distance. As a reminder of how close the slough was to saltwater, a seal briefly poked his head up near the far shore, stared me down, then swam around the next bend with the falling tide.

A fish rolled a short cast away. I had already rigged up a chartreuse Popsicle fly, an attractor pattern used to search out cruising fish, and stuck with it. I stripped out a few arm-lengths of line, false-cast, and shot the fly into the river. A light rain fell as I began stripping the fly back in short jerks. Halfway into the retrieve, the ghostly shape of a silver salmon could be seen tracking the fly, pushing a small wake. The fish literally ran out of water and veered away before it beached itself, leaving a boil that took several seconds to break up.

With all the self-control I could muster, and knowing that the very next cast with the Popsicle could result in a strike, I clipped off the fly and knotted on a Pink Pollywog.

The giant fly, as aerodynamic as a feather duster, made odd swooshing noises as I false-cast, before plopping it into the river thirty feet away. I twitched it back in short strips, causing it to gurgle and plop along the surface.

Suddenly the water humped up behind the fly. I continued retrieving. The hump developed into a full-blown bow wave, pursuing the Pollywog like an orca about to snatch a struggling sea lion. Then a large hooked jaw broke the surface, casually engulfed the fly, and turned away in a rush of water. The line came tight, and I had hooked my first silver salmon on a Pink Pollywog.

The fish wallowed for a few seconds, then tore away, churning the surface and spooking a dozen other fish from their respective lies. I made my way down the bank, surrendering line when the fish insisted. Eventually I slid a bright twelve-pound male salmon onto the bank, the Pollywog caught in the scissors of its jaw. I twisted the fly free, and slipped the fish back into the river, where it shot off, splashing me with its tail.

For the next hour and a half I could do no wrong. Silvers rose freely to the Pollywog, gulping it down as if it were their last meal. Once, when an errant cast splattered the Pollywog ten feet in front of me, a silver promptly came up and ate it. Another time, I walked up the creek a few yards and spotted a salmon holding motionless among submerged weeds. I cast, and watched the fish bolt for the Pollywog, then confidently slurp it down like a brown trout taking a Green Drake. Five minutes later, I slid a six-pound hen up the bank.

After landing a dozen salmon up to fifteen pounds, I actually began feeling twinges of relief when a fish would throw the fly prematurely, knowing I wouldn't have to wrestle the Pollywog from another angry silver's jaws. Stingy Alaska had suddenly turned into the well-meaning grandmother who fills your plate with another piece of blueberry pie, even though you're ready to burst.

But who can resist Grandma's pie, or the amazing gift of salmon rising to dry flies on every cast? So I plopped the Pink Pollywog into the river again, stripped twice, and immediately hooked another fighting, thrashing silver. *(September 22, 2002)*

A STEELHEAD CHALLENGE IN THE BRITISH COLUMBIA WILDERNESS

By Thomas McGuane

THE SHOOTING WOKE us up. A sow grizzly and her three large cubs had come into a camp and they were fighting over something in the yard, cuffing one another into the sides of the cabins. During the rest of the night, the guides did what they could to send them on their way, but nothing worked. Only sunrise helped. The four seemed consumed by guilt from their all-night party. They slipped into the brush on the west side of the camp and moments later were racing over the round stones of the river bar on their way out of Dodge.

It was exhilarating. They had been around before and in a previous year had even chewed up the proprietor's airplane. This year there were more than a few, dining on spawned-out salmon. It was an easy life on the verge of winter; but grizzlies did not require ease. If necessary, they would ascend the high, exposed scree slopes and snatch a mountain goat who thought he could safely watch the passing seasons in the valley below. It was rare for them to come into camp, and it certainly gave a new piquancy to late trips to the outhouse.

But this was the British Columbia wilderness and anything that made its contrast stark to our everyday world, like the grizzly bear, the raven, the wolf, or the eagle, was welcome. To the robust cubs backing around the cabins with garbage sacks and low growls, I wished to say, "Have at it."

I was here to fish for steelhead on one of the great angling rivers of the world, the Dean. It was my fourth trip, and as always with anadromous fish that return to spawn, the question was whether or not the fish were in.

With seagoing stocks everywhere, any delay in a run fills the angler with the fear that they may not come at all. River fish, which are subjected during part of their life cycle to the capacity and lawlessness of high-seas commercial fishing, face a serious question of survival these days.

The steelhead of each river system are a separate race with characteristics derived from deep time in a particular place. The Dean River fish are known for their speed and wild strength. They are particularly beautiful fish, too, deep-bodied and shapely. And they will come to a dry fly better than other strains, though the depth and clarity and prevailing temperatures of the river itself have much to do with this.

I caught a fish on the first day, then went into a long dry spell. Casting from daybreak to sundown, wading deep in clear green water as it swept past the gravel bars and wooded bases of mountains, is stirring exercise and with a floating line, the pleasures of casting alone are fulfilling. But by the time the second day rolled around and I had not moved a fish, I could feel the slight clench start, the clench that suggests you may never hook another steelhead if you cast for a thousand years.

I sat down on the rocky abutment of an old logging bridge where tame winter wrens explored for insects in the sunny cracked stones. Half of the second blank day was over, and I knew I was pressing.

For some reason hard to pin down, pressing won't work on steelhead. Covering the water is all-important, but so is fishing out each cast, mending and controlling fly speed. It's fly speed and the look of the fly making its small V-wake on the surface, things that come only by feel, that require energetic composure. An effective steelheader must control his temperament and stay on top of this matter of feel through long hours and disappointment and the wild conditions of Northwest coastal rivers.

I was dropped off at the top of the most beautiful steelhead pool I had ever seen. I had a moment to look the water over and tie on my favorite steelhead fly, the October Caddis.

There was a sparkling chute of white, boulder-strewn water at the head that quickly dissipated in the deep, flowing pool. The far side of the pool was a high rock wall covered with lichen. A ribbon falls descended its face and made a circle of bubbles in the water below. The tail-out of the pool was a shoal of small stones where the entire Dean River rushed toward the sea accompanied by impossibly rare music.

I began casting at the head of the pool, swept away by the beauty of this place and by the high sense of possibility this handsome water suggested to the angler. Very early on, a steelhead rose, took my fly lightly, released it, and disappeared.

Knowing that it may well have been the only take in a good long while, I felt a bit sunk, but went on casting in case the fish had not been touched and might move to my fly once more. Four casts later and the fish rose under the sparkling wake of the October Caddis, backed down a yard with it, and once again vanished.

It was too much. It was now almost technically hopeless; but since steelhead will come several times before they really line up on the fly, I kept casting. I tried to make the turnovers of the cast such that the fly always landed with a dead straight leader; this turned out to be the right thing, because on what must have been close to my last cast, the fish instantly rose and sucked down the fly.

I set the hook against a surge of power and the fish fought its way across the pool. It felt so strong that I recognized I did not have a particularly good chance of landing it. About halfway down the pool, the fish made a greyhounding jump and scared me with its size.

By the time we reached the tail-out, I knew I had to make a stand. If the fish got into the rapids, it was gone. I raised the pressure until the rod was bent into the cork handle. The steelhead held in the pool for several long moments, then yielded. I felt it turn and then miraculously come my way.

In a short time I slid the fish into a cove and tailed her, for it was a great big hen of about eighteen pounds, a beautiful slab of silver with a cloud of rosiness down her side. I removed the barbless hook and sent her on her way. I was ready for my next dry spell. *(December 1, 1991)*

A MEDITATION ON THE
FLY-FISHER IN WINTER

By Ernest Schwiebert

WINTER RAIN IS sifting through the trees.
We are still weeks away from fishing, except in our thoughts. Most streams were still unfrozen at Christmas, with tapestries of waterlogged leaves in the shallows, under brittle breakfast windowpanes of ice. Sedge larvae had discarded a few leafy skeletons, after they had shredded them, leaving only the pale lacework of their stems and veins.

The dark water appeared sepulchral and mute, becoming opaque and swollen with snowmelt. Cold wind rattled in the trees, under a raw pewter sky. The river seemed almost dead in its wintry shroud, but its entombment was merely an illusion, because the bottom sediment and cobble still teemed with unseen riches.

The weather became cold in January, until the icy trickle of our river was stilled; it was visible in few places, confined to sinkholes and runnels in its crystalline carapace of snow. Waterfalls were steadily transformed into staircases and balustrades, and the seepages of ledge-rock fissures became guttering organ pipes of ice.

There was little sign of fish, although they were certainly lurking in the wintry deeps. Many have spawned between Halloween and Christmas, and the ripe ova lie concealed in the winter gravel, ticking like miniature clocks. It will soon be time for their alevins to hatch. Most aquatic insects were partially grown at Halloween, while a few species are wintering as eggs. Their ova will also hatch before springtime. Other secrets of spring are stirring in the gritty, frostbitten earth.

Streams that remain open to winter fishing, like the Connetquot and Nissequogue and Carman's on Long Island, can surrender winter hatches from time to time, as the arctic cold loosens its chilling grip and we are permitted to enjoy the brief respite of a February thaw.

Some anglers are surprised to learn that fish will surface-feed in winter, and that some aquatic insects emerge well before April. Even more seem surprised that the biomass of aquatic insects in most streams is reaching its yearly apogee in March, as nymphs and larvae of an entire season's fly hatches approach maturity.

Fishing ends for most people when the trees are stripped of their summer's wealth, and regattas of leaves are scattered on the currents. The world seems to hibernate and doze, but its winter moratorium is not universal. Nymphs and larvae of a few aquatic insects display a surprising autumnal spurt of growth, as nights grow colder in October, and when conditions are right, such genera may emerge at midday throughout the winter.

Most of these winter insects are small, but two Eastern sedges are a happy exception. Hatching pupae of the Mottled Winter Sedge, called *Frenesia missa*, can be imitated with a dark sepia body, and a collar of dark partridge barbules in size 14. The unusual Winter Brown Sedge, called *Dolophilodes distinctus*, appears sporadically throughout the year. Females of its winter broods are often wingless and are found scuttling on snow cornices over the stream. Such emerging pupae are also imitated with a soft-hackled pattern of brown partridge and a body dubbing of rich chocolate.

I have often encountered midwinter emergences of stoneflies in fishable numbers, and have seen trout take them as they hatch from narrow runnels in the ice. Our Eastern species may range in size from a blackish 4-millimeter *Allocapnia* to reddish 12-millimeter specimens of *Strophopteryx*.

Other winter species include a medium-sized *Allocapnia* and the medium-sized February Reds and Winter Browns called *Nemoura* and *Taenipteryx*. Generic imitations of these dark winter nymphs should be rather sparsely dressed, in sizes 14 through 20. The basic palette of color should include rusty chestnut brown, dark chocolate, and black. These nymphs are rather poor swimmers, and fishing techniques should address such behavior and lack of agility.

Anglers who fish throughout the winter are also aware of the midday pupal drift and emergence of tiny *Chironomidae*. Such midge activity occurs throughout the year, although it is seldom noticed by anglers during the abundance of spring and summer. Midge pupae are often present in astonishing numbers, and in these seemingly barren months, they often have the limelight to themselves. Winter anglers on the Yellow Breeches and Little Juniata in central Pennsylvania usually fish a popular Griffith's Gnat in sizes 20 to 24.

"Might not think of dry flies when you're knee-deep in snow," David McMullen told me last winter at Spruce Creek. "But on a still winter afternoon, with enough sun to warm things up, you can take fish with a Griffith's Gnat."

There are other secrets in winter trout fishing, including the deployment of larger nymphs fished slow and deep, but these secrets should help when winter fish turn selective and feed on a single species. Now that some waters remain open, it is clear that winter offers some fishing.

And such activity is but a prelude of things to come. *(March 8, 2004)*

WARMWATERS

It is unclear why there is a relative dearth of stories about warmwater species, especially since largemouth bass are considered the most popular gamefish in the country. Panfish, too, enjoy an enormous following, with most anglers tracing their first-ever catch to a weedy pond and a school of willing bluegills.

Bass fishing may get a bad name from televised fishing tournaments that show fish after fish getting unceremoniously winched to the surface, chucked into a live-well, and later weighed on a soundstage straight out of The Price Is Right. The competitive bass-fishing mind-set also marginalizes those species that keep anglers "out of the money." Sunfish—even goliath two-pound bluegills—don't win bass tournaments. And pickerel devolve into slimy trash fish that bite through your line.

But you wouldn't know any of this from reading "Outdoors," where canoes, creaky rowboats, or even rubber boots hold the line against gleaming, high-powered bass rigs. Green sunfish—diminutive panfish that may never reach a pound—become objects of obsession. Two-pound pickerel are gladly kept and eaten (but carefully deboned first). And sometimes the water erupts as a five-pound largemouth bass slams a surface bug. When the fish is eventually brought to the boat, it is quietly released, or occasionally tossed into a cooler, a wayward loon or a bullfrog as the only witness.

SEASON OF THE

BIGMOUTH APPROACHES

By Nick Lyons

TROUT ARE MORE beautiful. Salmon leap higher, more explosively. So do tarpon, which are stronger and larger. Bonefish make far longer runs. Bluegill the size of your palm, pound for pound, fight harder. Their smallmouth cousins receive more attention, especially from those who pursue them with a fly rod. A northern pike, looking like some Neolithic monster as it swipes at a fly you have jerked out of the water, brings greater shock and surprise.

Why, then, as another season is about to begin, do my dreams, memories, and expectations turn to largemouth bass? They have no rose moles on their flanks; they are not fussy about some minuscule plat du jour; even the largest seldom take me near my backing. Snobbishly, I do not like the company they keep; most of the folks who fish for bass do so from god-awful spangled boats, using words hard on my tongue, like *hawg* and *structure*. They use purple plastic worms or spinnerbaits or live golden shiners bigger than most trout I catch, often in hot competition with their neighbors, and I leave every competitive bone I have on the dock.

The fish looks positively mean and ugly — bronze-green, chunky, with a big mouth and little heart for a fight. The largemouth bass is a kind of dormant or slowly prowling predator with a skulking, genuinely antisocial attitude. It likes dark, gloomy parts of a lake, and once hooked, it gives you a jump or two, a sturdy run of not much duration, then a heavy shaking of its big head. If it is a big bass — say, six or seven pounds — it takes a bit more pumping to haul it in.

But, oh, how I love the ugly old bigmouth bass. I love the fish and I love to fish for it in a specific way, with outsize fly tackle, bugs the size of bats, cablelike leaders, from a rowboat, along a shoreline whenever I possibly can. If I must, I will fish for them in the middle of the day — and I always get one or two because there are always a few largemouth bass in the shallows, whatever the books and the experts say, under some roots or an abandoned dock, or at the edge of some lily pads. They like shade and they can get it in quiet shallow water, along with an occasional dragonfly or a frog, an injured bluegill fry or a careless minnow.

Mornings, of course, can be spectacular, when there is not more than the faintest touch of light in the sky, when the biggest fish have been on the prowl since dusk after a nighttime of foraging. But I simply cannot get up at that hour anymore. No, I like best to fish for them at dusk and slightly afterward — an hour or two at a time, looking for one good fish, perhaps a few.

I love to fish for them in an old rowboat, with oarlocks that creak but will not let an oar slip free, so I can take my hands from them to cast and know that they will still be there. I love to fish for them alone, or with a friend who knows what we are after, even if he is baffled by my gear. One of us will row, with quiet, alternating tugs, parallel to the shore when the lake has gone calm and the first thin mist begins to rise. The rower keeps the boat sixty or eighty feet from the shoreline, or from the edges of pickerelweed or lily pads or deadfalls. I will cast in my huge bug, the line and rod heavy as they reach back and then forward.

I use a ten-foot rod for a weight-forward No. 11 line, from

which I cut three feet from the front taper and tie on an eight-foot, ten-pound-test leader, untapered. The bug, with a deer-hair body and clumps of yellow-dyed impala tail extending like four legs, is no less than four or five inches across. It waffles out a lot less delicately than I would like, then settles. I twitch it once or twice, then let it sit, and sit. Then I wiggle it a little by keeping my rod tip facing the bug and nearly touching the water and by tugging at the line. I chug it a little. Then I tug at the line so the bug sputters and throws some water. I have no fixed formula. I like to innovate.

And this is the moment I love best. It contains, in its special suspense, the reason I love to fish for largemouth bass — teasing a fish up, drawing it to my big bug like a turkey hunter calling in his bird, waiting, watching the dormant bug, connected to the bug by eye and line, waiting, manipulating the bug with a little hop and dance on a still lake, the bug creasing the flat surface near an old dock. And then raising the line from the surface with as little disturbance as possible, pushing it behind me, and casting again.

If my companion is a trout fisherman, he will smile and shake his head. It may seem pretty heavy-handed to him. He may even be as snobbish to me and this monstrosity of a bug as I am to a purple plastic worm. Snobbery, by nature, is less objectively hierarchical than arbitrary. I am sure there is nothing inherently low about a purple plastic worm or a big, clumsy bug, but thinking in certain ways makes it so.

I imagine that on a seventeenth cast, right before dark, having tried a patch of lily pads and long gray deadfall, now to within an inch of a great stump, the water erupts, implodes, with a curved back, a crater of water, and silver everywhere, and I strike quickly, lean into the fish, and soon have it in, my left thumb in its jaw, pressing down.

"I can't believe you raised a fish on a bug that big," my friend says, his eyes wide.

"The bass is called 'the lip that swims,'" I tell him. "Like me, it likes a big plate of food."

"But on a bug like that?"

The season is upon us, and I have a dozen bass trips planned. I try to think of what response I could make to my trout friend, and all I can summon is, "Well, the fish has got a verrry big mouth." *(June 16, 2003)*

AS THE SEASON GETS COLDER,
THE BASS GET WISER

By Robert H. Boyle

B ETWEEN EARLY OCTOBER and the end of November, when the largemouth season ended for
the year in New York State, it was, to paraphrase
Dickens, the best of times, and sometimes the most frustrating
of times. Provided water temperatures were right, it was the
best of times, because the fish were at their feistiest, feeding
avidly to build up the energy reserves needed to carry them to
spring.

Three largemouths I caught on a lightly fished lake on
October 9, a balmy Indian summer day, were already plumper
than their brethren of a month previous. Filleted, skinned,
soaked in milk, lightly floured, and sautéed in butter, they
were a heavenly mouthful for me, my wife, and a dinner guest.

But when cold weather dropped the water temperature
into the high forties, the bass moved to deeper water and became slower to take a lure. The body temperature of a largemouth is approximately the same as that of water; when the
temperature drops, so does the bass's metabolism, and it has
less need to feed. In the winter, with ice covering a lake, a bass
may feed only once in two weeks, if that.

❖   ❖   ❖

Largemouths are essentially muggers, lying in wait to engulf
any live prey, be it dragonfly, minnow, or duckling. All the

bass I caught during the month of October up to the twenty-eighth of the month were within twenty feet of the shoreline, ready to ambush small sunnies seeking refuge in the shallows.

I took the fish on a spinning rod with four-pound-test lines, using a red-and-white Silly Jig with a tail of two-inch feathers. How this seductive jig got its peculiar name is not known, but it is shaped like a slender football and weighs an eighth of an ounce. Unlike a ball-head jig that goes up and down, it is a swimming jig.

Seth Rosenbaum of the Bronx introduced me to the Silly Jig thirty-four years ago, when he used it to catch striped bass in the Hudson River. All told, Rosenbaum has taken more than a hundred species of fish on it, ranging from brook trout to a world-record Atlantic bonito. "The Silly Jig can be a bait-fish, or possibly a shrimp or a squid or whatever I want it to be," he said. "I can bounce it, move it sideways, up and down, or backward. It can do almost anything you want it to."

Rosenbaum joined me one October afternoon at the lake to fish for largemouth, and in the two hours before sunset he caught the limit of five on a diving Rapala plug. He kept only one, but he could have taken all of them home. Unlike trout fishing, the mantra of "catch and release" does not hold for largemouths, as the late Dr. George W. Bennett of the Illinois Natural History Survey demonstrated in study after study.

My personal bass guru, Bennett ran his own experimental largemouth lake for years. Anglers had to check in and out, keep every bass caught regardless of size, and note bait and lure used.

Data he collected and analyzed showed that artificial lures were more effective than live bait, and more bass were caught on underwater plugs than on floating plugs. But, most important, the data showed that bass quickly learned to avoid capture.

Anglers caught more bass the morning of the first day of

the season than they did later in the afternoon, and the catch continued to decline for several days afterward, before it finally leveled off. By the end of the season, the average fisherman's catch rate was one pound of bass for every seven hours of fishing.

Of course, skill played a part. One fisherman caught a pound of bass for every one hour and forty-five minutes he fished, while an equally enthusiastic angler took almost twelve hours to catch a pound. What made the difference? The successful fisherman tried methods and lures with which the bass were likely to be unfamiliar.

When fishermen complained that there were no more large bass in the eighteen-acre lake, George drained a two-acre pond that had been fished heavily for several years and found forty-five legal-sized bass, with a dozen of them weighing three to six pounds.

All in all, George found that when fishing pressure amounts to more than sixty man-hours per acre a year, the bass have been educated and are too smart to be caught. So what's an angler to do? Anglers in New York, New Jersey, and Connecticut are fortunate indeed. New York City's reservoir system in Westchester and Putnam Counties is too vast to get that kind of pressure, and it contains some humongous bass.

All that is needed to try for them is a state license and a Water Supply Fishing Permit good for five years from the city's Department of Environmental Protection.

But now, you'll have to wait till next year. *(November 30, 1997)*

STRUGGLING TO MASTER

A NEW FISHING LANGUAGE

By James Gorman

I WILL NOT say that my first fish on a jig and pig was as momentous as my first fish on a fly, but it was satisfying nonetheless. It was a fat little crappie (or calico bass) that took the lure in the weeds while I was pretending to be a bass fisherman.

A few years ago, I spent a day with a real bass fisherman, a professional, watching him work Louisiana bayous with dexterous flips of a jig that he would drop into the water within a half inch of whatever patch of weeds or dock or submerged log he picked.

The jig had a lead head and a synthetic skirt and was baited with a bit of flexible, wiggly fluorescent plastic slipped on the hook like an old-fashioned pork rind (thus jig and pig). After each cast he would give it a bump or two, and then reel in the lure for another quick flip. Or he would slam the rod back to set the hook and pull in a bass.

Naturally, I had to get myself a bass outfit, a rod that would work for casting or those quick little flips, a bait-casting reel with an antibacklash mechanism (required for fly-fishermen flirting with bass tackle), and some high-tech, no-stretch fluorocarbon line.

Trout fishing has been compared to religion, Presbyterianism in particular. It has its roots in England, land of warm beer and chilly manners. Bass fishing is what you do when you are not going to church. It is purely American, with its roots in the South, the land of chilly beer and hot barbecue.

Sometimes, when I am walking through the fishing aisles at one of the big Marts, K or Wal, and I see a package of purple, gold-flecked plastic worms and imitation slugs, with their special scents and "worm salt," I feel that I am missing something, like being in a restaurant in a foreign country and not knowing exactly what *tête de veau* is. (Extremely good shark bait is what it is.)

So I try, fitfully, to master a new fishing language. I get out my bait-casting outfit, study the difference in putting a plastic worm on a Carolina and a Texas rig (interestingly, the Carolinas and Texas also differ on barbecue), and try to catch fish.

But I have always lacked confidence. As many a fishing expert has noted, you catch far more fish with lures or flies that you have confidence in. When you have caught a lot of fish on a hare's-ear nymph, you may do well with it even though another pattern might be better, because you work it thoroughly.

I decided to give my bass rig another try on a trip my father and I had decided to take on Mudge Pond in Sharon, Connecticut. I had never been there, but it has a reputation for being a good small bass lake with all sorts of other fish.

New rivers can be intimidating. New lakes can be tough to take on. But ponds or small lakes are welcoming. I'm not sure how the line is drawn, but if the shores on all sides always seem within comfortable reach, that is the size I am talking about. I took an old aluminum canoe. My father took an electric trolling motor and we met at the pond, which is tucked away in one of the prettiest parts of the state.

It was the Monday after Father's Day, and until the late afternoon there were no other boats on the 206-acre pond, which has heavy weeds, a beach at one end, and few houses.

Once we got out of the weeds, we drifted and motored and drifted, trying different spots and different techniques. I took a fly rod for comfort, and quickly started to get a lot of hits on small yellow poppers. They were some of the fattest pumpkinseeds I have seen, beautiful-colored, spunky panfish.

My father was using a diving orange-and-black bumble-bee on a spinning rod, and he pulled in a small bass and several crappie. The day was warm, with a breeze. The fish, though small, were biting. The weather threatened occasionally, and even produced some showers and thunder late in the day, but the shore was always close enough. All in all, it was lazy and relaxed fishing.

I switched to my bass rig. Naturally, I hoped to catch a monster, but I realized after talking to a local fisherman at the end of the day that we would have had to plumb deeper water for big bass. Later in the season, he said, top-water lures worked well, but for now, plastic worms on the bottom were best.

That seemed contrary to common sense. I thought in the hot weather the bass would go deeper, but when I checked the description of the pond that the Connecticut Department of Environmental Protection has on the Web, I found a possible explanation. In the summer the waters of the pond become stratified, warmer water on top, cooler water below, with little mixing. Dissolved oxygen does not reach the deeper water, and the fish move closer to the surface.

I did not really mind not catching the big ones, though. When I tossed the jig into some weeds, gave it a little bounce, and had a hit, the rod and reel were transformed in my hands. It is an old angling chestnut that you fish best with tackle you have confidence in. Until I had made the bait-casting outfit work, I was unable to use it diligently. I would give up too quickly.

One fish gave me confidence, like the first successful conversation in a foreign language. After that, I was diligent. I figured out the proper way to cast (that had definitely been holding me back), and I tried other sorts of lures. I caught fish with the jig, I caught fish with a plastic worm. Actually it may have been a slug, or an invertebrate from another planet, but it was plastic, it smelled funny, and I fished it with a Texas rig. And I caught a bass, a small one, but a bass nonetheless, on a spinner bait, a V-shaped contraption with spinners and a skirt.

I cannot say that I am giving up fly-fishing, but I now look on my bait-casting setup as an effective fishing tool. I do not consider myself fluent in Bass, but I know a few phrases. Plus, I found a new pond that I know I will fish again. Maybe late in summer when the bass are coming to the top. Then I will use a buzz bait. *(June 30, 2002)*

IN THE DEPTHS OF CENTRAL PARK, FISHING ON THE FLY

By Paul Guernsey

I RECENTLY DISCOVERED that the way to shock many New Yorkers was to tell them I planned to fly-fish in Central Park. They invariably thought I was joking, and after I finally convinced them, they were incredulous. Of all the strange things that occur in the park, fly-fishing seems the least imaginable to a lot of people.

But there are largemouth bass in the park's eight ponds, and some of them get quite large. The only permission you need to go after them is a fishing license.

The Urban Angler Fly Shop on 25th Street arranged for me to explore Central Park with a man named Edwin Valentin, who fly-fishes there frequently and sometimes agrees to show his favorite spots to visitors.

I started out by fishing by myself at Turtle Pond, near 60th Street. Not only was I unsuccessful with my deer-hair popper, but I quickly discovered that I had to be very careful with my backcast since not only were people constantly passing behind me, but many of them froze just behind my right shoulder in a trance of either fascination or terror.

Then Edwin appeared. He was an energetic young man in shorts and a thigh-length Daffy Duck T-shirt. He carried an inexpensive fly rod, and his baseball cap was stuck full of colorful bass flies, including several of his own imaginative invention.

"Okay, you can't use a popper here," he told me. "Never work. They're always feeding under the water. Leeches are better." I was about to change flies when he said, "It's better on 105th Street anyway. I caught a nineteen-inch bass there Thursday."

❖   ❖   ❖

Edwin told me that he'd grown up in Bushwick, and after the first of his two children was born, several years ago, he'd relocated to Manhattan. He worked part-time repairing bicycles and doing odd jobs, and fishing whenever he could. He is a self-taught fly-fisher and fly-tier, and he picks up new patterns and tying techniques in the books at Barnes & Noble.

"Before I had a fly-tying vise, I used to hold the hook in my toes," he told me.

As we passed the reservoir, he said a police scuba diver who'd once had to search the bottom for a body had told him he'd seen bass so big they scared him. Now Edwin, a catch-and-release angler, can't stop dreaming about those fish. "If that fence ever comes down, I'll be the first one there," he said.

Finally, near 105th Street, at a willow-shaded pond called the Pool, Edwin pointed out a sizable largemouth loitering near the shore. "Here, put this on," he said, and gave me a black leech imitation from his hat. "Throw it right in front of him and strip it slow."

I did as he said, making repeated casts, including a back-cast that ended up wrapped around a lamppost. But the bass ignored my offering and finally disappeared.

"They're spawning right now," Edwin said. "You have to make them mad." It was a hot day, though, and I began to suspect that the water might be too warm for even a spawning bass to expend much energy.

❖   ❖   ❖

During the next hour we found several fish, some of them good ones. But although we changed flies frequently — to ever more improbable colors — we couldn't get them to take. Finally, Edwin did hook one, proving that a Central Park largemouth will take a properly — and persistently — presented fly. I myself hooked only a sunken tire.

Then we headed for the Harlem Meer. As we traveled, Edwin pointed out several examples of the urban hunting and gathering that takes place in Central Park. He showed me a homeless man trying to untangle a snarl of monofilament. "Fishing for catfish," he said. "They eat ducks, too."

We also spotted a couple of women stripping mulberries from bushes near an entrance to the park, and Edwin told me other anglers scoured the park's trickling brooks for the resident crayfish — some of which have blue shells.

We reached the Harlem Meer, where the water was cleaner and deeper than anything we had seen so far. Central Park officials later told me this was the best place in the park for bass. But the day was even hotter now, and we saw no more fish. Still, I was thoroughly satisfied with the outing: Edwin had given me a perspective on both New York and Central Park that I couldn't have gotten anywhere else. *(July 29, 1995)*

SMALLMOUTH BASS HELP
IN ENDING A BRIEF SLUMP

By James Gorman

I T'S MIDSUMMER on the Housatonic in Connecticut. The heat is up, the water is down, and the trout are holding in cooler areas where feeder streams enter the river. You can spot these so-called thermal refuges by the signs that tell you not to fish within 100 feet of the tributaries.

There's no shortage of insect life. The caddis flies, in particular, are bouncing around everywhere. But the fish are asleep in the shade.

The trout, that is. The smallmouth bass are wide awake. Bathtub temperatures (in the mid-seventies) make them feel peckish, and it is Article 1 of the smallmouth creed that all things great and small are food, and that no fish ever grew big by limiting its carnivorous ambitions to creatures that fit into its mouth. They call them smallies, but their hearts and appetites are huge. I love smallmouth bass.

I spent an afternoon and evening fishing for smallies on the Housatonic last week, and at one point when the action slowed down, I tied on the biggest, ugliest wet fly I had in my box, a creation with feathers, fur, chenille, and rubber legs that I believe is meant to imitate the unholy spawn of a stonefly and one of those worm guys from *Men in Black II*.

I drifted it through a deep run and caught a bass that had ambitions to be five inches long but hadn't fulfilled those ambitions yet. The fly it chomped on was about three inches long.

If it isn't obvious already, I should say that I have a big soft spot for smallmouths. The first fish I ever caught on a fly rod was a smallmouth bass, on a lake in Maine. I was thirteen and had spent all spring practicing casting in my backyard according to a pamphlet that came with my new fly rod.

I admit that smallmouth bass are often easier to catch than trout. In fact, I went smallmouth fishing partly because I've been in a bit of a slump lately. I hit bottom in Montana in June. I went on a float trip down the Madison River during the salmon fly hatch and did not catch a fish. (I could hear the announcer saying, "You know, it's painful to watch. He's trying so hard but he's all off balance, his weight is too far back, and it's like he's not seeing the ball.")

Actually, I did foul-hook a whitefish, which I believe looked at me with its suckerlike mouth and said something scornful and unprintable. The guide didn't hear it.

I also hooked several trout that got away and had a fair number of hits, but not one trout came into the boat. When the guide dropped me off at the fly shop, he couldn't face going inside. I promised him not to print his name.

Something was seriously wrong. The guide told me my casting was adequate, that I was mending line well enough to get a decent drift, as evidenced by the few hits I had. There were two problems, he said. One was that the section of river we floated was maybe a day or two past its peak, so the fish were full instead of crazily voracious. The other problem — my problem — was that I just wasn't setting the hook.

We were fishing big nymphs on a nine-foot leader, with a smaller nymph on a dropper, casting twenty to thirty feet over currents of different speed. The trout had been seeing a lot of fishing pressure, and had tasted a lot of artificial flies, and they would sense a mouthful of feathers quickly, and spit it out. The trick, as with most nymph fishing, was to start to set the hook almost before you saw a bump on the strike indicator. My timing was off.

❊   ❊   ❊

When I came back from Montana, I thought I needed some time in the minors — a rehab assignment. I'm not saying smallmouth bass are lesser fish than trout. But they are less picky. They do like to slam the living daylights out of flies. And they don't get as much pressure from the *River Runs Through It* crowd as those mouth-weary Montana browns.

I started out fishing a weighted crayfish imitation, dead drift, just like a salmon fly, but on a short leader (five feet of braided sinking leader, and a foot of ten-pound-test saltwater tippet, as suggested by the salesman at the fly shop). Shortly after stepping into the river I hooked my first fish, which escaped. No pressure, I told myself, no pressure.

And indeed there wasn't. I prowled the warm river, in places ankle-deep, looking for runs and holes, drifting the crayfish somewhere near the bottom. With the shorter leader and harder takes, I caught fish. I began to feel that I knew what was happening underwater, where the fly was, and which movements of the strike indicator were meaningful.

The fish I caught weren't big, but several were ten inches or longer, so they were fun to catch, since smallies fight as if they have no idea of their size.

As I was wading, several people on inner tubes floated by, one of them with a fly rod. I saw him later at the end of his run, and he said that even though he had lost all his flies when they fell out of a pocket, an angler on the river had given him a fly and he had caught five or six bass.

That's a method I hadn't thought of—bathing suit and inner tube. Just stop when you like, or wedge yourself against a rock and drop a fly into the water. If you're not in the mood, just let your hand drift in the water and splash yourself when you get hot.

I love smallmouths. *(July 14, 2002)*

NATURE HAS A WAY OF
FINDING US ALL

By Craig Springer

W E ARE WHAT we cross paths with — not what we
seek out, but what takes hold of us. These associations
create our core. They become the essence of our being.

A little stream grabbed a hold on me and became a mean-
dering baseline, an anchor point from which I would take all
bearings for things to come. Creek chub, smallmouth bass, and
green sunfish: they caught me. And it was angling for them
that immersed me in a narrative with the stream and lands that
drained into it.

Four Mile Creek heads among the uplands near the Ohio-
Indiana line in hills left behind by retreating glaciers. Tiny
rivulets formed in the folds of the land, mostly cleared for corn
and beans. One rivulet begets two and so on, forming Four
Mile; the creek gathers them as it glides downhill, cutting over
ancient glacial till carried far from the north.

In these quiet waters, damselflies dimple their metallic blue tails
on the smooth glides as their eggs drop into the creek. They
waft erratically on the wing as if they have no purpose or care.
Save for entering the maw of a kingbird, they probably do not.

Four Mile's erosive forces elbow into the foot of a hill, un-
dercutting the banks that stay stitched together by sycamore
roots. In the shade of the undercut, the shards of turquoise —

101

little green sunfish — are there waiting for the groceries to come to them. It is a good strategy for making a living in a creek. Find a place to hide from herons and kingfishers, stay in shade so unsuspecting minnows cannot see you, and sit there and wait for food to come drifting.

The strategy must work. Green sunfish live naturally all over the Midwest. And that speaks to their durability in extremes, not to mention their capacity to procreate. They look to me like a mix of smallmouth bass, bluegill, and rock bass — like an animal confused, not knowing which evolutionary trajectory to take. A big gape allows green sunfish to eat most anything they want; bats and shrews have shown up in their gullets, but bugs are the favored fare.

Among upland streams in the Midwest, the smallmouth bass is king, the green sunfish a mere commoner.

But the literature professor Marcus Selden Goldman, who ninety years ago fished Four Mile Creek while at Miami of Ohio, strikes a chord in his book *In Praise of Little Fishes:* "The crowd in its ignorance deems it manly and impressive to catch crappies and bluegill, but scorns anything called 'sunfish.' The result of this attitude is that only seasoned and thoughtful anglers know or care to know how to identify the different species of sunfishes."

I don't disagree, but I know of no one who would plan a fishing trip around green sunfish. And I must admit I probably wouldn't, either. But I would like to see Four Mile again. It's a yen in part for yesterday; a yearning to reacquaint myself with that baseline, the habitat where I came of age. Neil Young said it perfectly in song: "In my mind I still need a place to go. All my changes were there."

Too many summers have slipped downstream. But still, in my mind's eye a diving beetle lumbers to the surface for air and a blue damselfly on a water willow moves its wings lightly and gracefully. The sodden smell of sticky mud fills my head. I can feel in my forearm the sudden tear of a smallmouth bass taking off with a spinner. And I wouldn't mind the light plodding of one of those little cyan sunfish with a mouth big enough to take whatever it can.

A creek is more than a place for bass and bream, warblers and wood ducks. It is a habitat for people. Habitat conservation benefits people. Creeks course through people. A tall, fat, gray-green sycamore on a shady undercut bend grows naked with age. Slow-moving dark water spattered with yellow sunlight pours over fossil-littered limestone slabs. In the shelter of a pool in a tangle of roots, little fish wait there, the wild consequences of time preserved in living turquoise shards. *(January 23, 2005)*

LETTING NATURE WORK, WITH

AID FROM AN EARTHMOVER

By Nick Lyons

WOODSTOCK, N.Y. — My ambition, simpler than Thoreau's, was merely to build a small pond to sit near, look at, fish in. I'd bought the property several years ago, on a hillside, and I remembered that Thoreau had said, "It is well to have some water in your neighbourhood, to give buoyancy to and float the earth."

This made sense to an old fisherman whose summer house had no water in the immediate neighborhood. So I decided to dig a pond in the rocky soil on the slope downhill from the house. The land needed a pond, and so did I.

I ignored my wife's question — "But don't you need water to build a pond?" — and found a little flat land, greener than its surroundings. I'd have gotten a dowser, but there was only one place to dig anyway.

So in October I applied for a building permit, showed the inspector where the berm and swale would go, listened impatiently as he advised that the soil had too many rocks and too little clay and would hold water for only four months of the year, and hired an excavator.

The excavator's father came each morning at seven and sat in the big Cat with a cigar in the same corner of his mouth all day, moving rock and earth, reshaping the land, happy to be out of retirement, his wife happy to have him out of the house. Back and forth he chugged, plunging the claw down, then turning uphill and depositing the earth.

In a week the excavator and his father — driving up and back across the hillside below me, pulling out a few trees by the roots, burying some, moving tons of Catskill rock, building a new hillside — had dug me a beautiful little amoeba-shaped hole, too far for me to cast across, with a long berm to keep the water from flooding down the far hill, a swale to bring rain runoff into the pond, and an exit should the water rise to its full height, should I be so lucky. When the pond was twelve feet deep, I felt the water oozing out of the aquifer on the north side of the hole. It was clear and cold and floated my spirits.

At first it was a nifty hole, with a little brown puddle in the deepest portion, as if someone had put too much milk in the coffee. But it wasn't a pond yet. I know the difference between a pond and a hole. I know a hole when I see one.

The excavator said it would fill, and it did. With November rains, it swelled to full flower and overflowed, and then when it snowed, it looked lovely and pure in the pocket of the hill. But by February it had sunk in upon itself, the snow like the skin of a dead cow I once saw, shrunken, everything alive in it done in by coyotes and maggots, its skin sucked in so it looked like a deflated balloon.

"Wouldn't it look better if there were some grasses and trees?" my wife said in March, adding that by high summer it would make a perfectly lovely mosquito farm.

As the spring progressed, some grasses grew, a little water a dowser might have found welled up from the ground above the pond, and several well-meaning friends brought gifts, like the three wise men, from their own fecund waters. They brought all manner of living things: minnows (more than a hundred of them), golden shiners (a dozen or so), sunfish (of various sizes), koi (three), a painted turtle, a couple of frogs, half a dozen pollywogs, and even three extraordinarily lucky largemouth bass.

The bass were large and would feast gloriously for at least a month. But what then? For it's early July now and I am beginning to worry whether, having imposed my will on this once-wooded acre below the house, transformed the materials of the earth in a way I thought would be better for them, that they would like better, while I had water to sit near and fish in, the pond will survive its first year.

Is it a muddy pit, after all, or a pond? Will it flourish or die? Are the bass in for a death far worse — and much slower — than the quick demise they dish out? For it's clear by now that the hole doesn't hold its water. Its color is pure mud. The turtle seems to have lit out for better parts already. One koi has vanished, perhaps as a meal for the raccoon whose tracks are everywhere or that great fisher of fish, the blue heron that vacuumed my neighbor's pond and has now set its eye on mine. I wish the nature of the land didn't seem so unnatural. I wish I could stop brooding that I should have learned to live without anything to float my land.

And each day, as the waterline slips lower and the heron looks happier, I have a more vivid vision of the inevitable drawdown in August, of the fish gasping for air, boiling slowly, the hawks and crows circling for their share of the spoils, mud everywhere, mosquitoes everywhere, some with West Nile virus. I have nightmares about this colossal mess I've made, and keep debating with myself whether to stay the course or net out the remaining fish, return them to their donors, and fill the pit with earth and rock to the top of the berm.

Still, last evening, after a light rain, the water looked a bit clearer, not much lower, and the pond was lousy with life: newts, frogs jumping in as I came close, a school of tiny, newly hatched bass, sunfish digging their pancake-shaped beds and, sideways, depositing their eggs. All the creatures seemed to like their new home. So maybe I should wait and let this new nature take its course, and see what happens. Maybe it just won't end as catastrophically as I'm positive it will. *(July 4, 2004)*

LOOKING FOR PICKEREL AND

RENEWING LIFE AT CAMP

By Nelson Bryant

S ALMON STREAM LAKE, ME. — The temperature was about 45 degrees and a steady rain was falling as Ruth Kirchmeier and I paddled down Salmon Stream to our camp on Salmon Stream Lake in the early afternoon during the first week in June.

We were cold and wet but delighted that we were getting all our gear and clothing plus food for nine days to camp in one canoe trip, and we knew that we would be settled in before darkness descended over the rain-shrouded lake. Just past the halfway point to the camp, a young beaver swam out from shore to survey us. Displaying no fear, it floated alongside our canoe about fifteen feet away, then slipped under the water and went back to dining on the bark of alder saplings.

Around the next bend, a female moose was browsing on aquatic plants. She watched us calmly, vegetation dangling from her mouth, and let us paddle to within fifty feet before lurching ashore and — surprisingly agile once on hard ground — disappearing under dark spruces.

The top of a big spruce snapped off by a windstorm had fallen into the water on the river side of the camp where we usually beach our canoe. We worked our way around it and in an hour had everything under cover.

About fifty percent of the peninsula on which our camp is located is heath or bog where cranberries, leatherleaf, pitcher plants, loosestrife, and other denizens of wet places thrive. The camp is on a site once occupied by a commercial sporting camp that flourished in the early 1900s, and is the only structure on the mile-long lake.

While Ruth put our food away, swept the camp, and made our bed, I got some damp kindling ignited with the help of birch bark and a dash of cooking oil, and soon had a good fire going in our little raised-hearth fireplace. After getting the propane gas appliances — stove, refrigerator, and lights — functioning, I donned hip boots, grabbed my chain saw, and, water flying, cut up the offending spruce and cleared the boat landing.

The temperature dropped into the low thirties that night, but the rising sun streaming in through the glass doors and windows the next morning and a lively blaze in the fireplace soon had the place comfortable. As we were eating breakfast, two loons were busily fishing out front as a lone bald eagle soared above them.

In a typical week I seldom see more than two other anglers on Salmon Stream Lake, and most of the time I have the fishing to myself. I don't experience the excitement encountered when wooing glorious Atlantic salmon in Canada or huge, acrobatic tarpon in Costa Rica, but I am deeply content. Solitude with a cherished friend is precious.

The shallow lake holds chain pickerel, white and yellow perch, and smallmouth bass. I have taken several bass in excess of five pounds from it, nearly all in the boulder-strewn outlet channel. On my most recent trip I wanted to go there right away, but a gale-force south wind was howling up the lake, and trying to paddle there would have been foolhardy, perhaps impossible.

I settled on going after pickerel in an area close to camp that was partly protected from the wind. On my second cast, a twenty-inch pickerel streaked from his hideaway among a cluster of lily pads and engulfed my plug, and in a half hour I had two more of the same size. The three pickerel were all we needed for supper, so I headed back to camp.

Pickerel, which have firm, sweet-tasting white flesh, are not favored as a food fish by many anglers because of fine, free-floating, Y-shaped bones along the backbone, but those bones can be removed with judicious knife work. I usually roll the skinned fillets in yellow cornmeal that has been seasoned with salt, pepper, and basil, and pan-fry them in bacon fat. This time around, I also had slices of raw pickerel — enhanced with soy sauce, wasabi mustard, and pickled ginger — for lunch.

A few days after we arrived at camp, my older son, Steve, and his wife, Lissa, who live in Bradford, Maine, visited us for a day. Steve and I fished for pickerel in Salmon Stream, keeping half a dozen of them that were over twenty inches. He used a large, single-hooked spinnerbait the entire time, and caught more fish than I.

Other visitors that day included Ed Rush of Sherman Station, Maine, and his nephew Steve Rush, of Lake Hopatcong, New Jersey. The elder Rush, now in his eighties, said that in the 1920s his father, Joe, and his father's brother Fred took over, via a lease, the sporting camp building. They maintained it for family and friends until the 1970s, he said.

During most of our visit, strong winds kept us from exploring the lake by canoe, but on one blustery day we paddled a short distance up the west side of the peninsula before being forced to take shelter on a small island.

Ashore on the island, we noticed a loon bouncing in the rough water on the windward side about twenty yards away, where it remained, watching us, during our hourlong stay. Surmising that it had a nest and a mate on the island, we didn't move about and departed as soon as possible — our lightly laden twenty-foot canoe yawing down the waves and spray flying — to avoid disturbing it further. *(June 20, 2004)*

A SKINNY LITTLE GIRL,
A FISHING ROD, A BLUEGILL

By Nick Lyons

SHE WAS PRECISELY the kind of little girl I would have fallen madly in love with, had I been six or seven and not her grandfather. She was skinny, with blond curly hair cut short, gangly when she ran, restless with dull adult talk, a chatterbox herself, crazy for her grandfather's stories, her two front teeth gone and paid for, not nearly so shy of seeing worms for the first time that she would not hold one.

In short, she was the perfect prospect for a fishing pal, and I had known this for a long time and had laced my letters to her with bluegill, trout, bass, hooks, bobbers. I tested a rod by asking her to pull on the line. I was lousy with indirection, determined not to force her, determined not to let the unintelligible jargon of fly-fishing wreck my plot, as I had let it spoil everything with her three uncles.

I would have to wait six years for her four-month-old brother, Tom, and he might not like worms so well. So I was laying something of a groundwork in the piscatorial direction, through innuendo and cunning. I was no fool. I would not force anyone anymore. I was not at all sure why we want those we love to love what we love, but forcing never helped.

"Of course you're forcing her," my shrewd daughter said. "Don't you see yourself at all, Dad? Leave my little girl alone."

"Maybe she'll love fishing," I said quietly.

"It's a perfectly good thing to do, this fishing of yours, but some people just don't like it, Dad — and no one likes it as much as you do," she said. "That may be hard for you to imagine, but it's true."

"I have a gut feeling about your little girl," I said. "She's got — "

"Piscatorial potential," she said. "I know. I know, Dad."

But I backed away anyway and mentioned fish not at all over the summer until a few weeks ago. The temperature got up to 104 degrees near Woodstock, New York, the creeks were dry, the nearest lake low, and I knew I would have to make some dramatic moves or the season would be over. At seventy, you reckon the number of seasons left.

No flies this time. No rod for me, so I could not possibly rage around rivers demonically possessed, fishing for twelve or fourteen hours at a time while my sons grew hopelessly bored, began to throw stones, and their sister, Lara's mother, had to advise them, "Be good — or Dad will put you in a story." No. The heyday of the blood, piscatorially speaking, was over. No entomology this time; no 6X leaders; no cul-de-canard winging; no big-name rivers with trout so snobby they sneered at the poorly presented fly.

❧　　❧　　❧

We began in my backyard with a rusted can, a shovel, and the hunt for worms with each spadeful of earth turned. I remembered the ritual well. If I was going to make a hunter-fisher-gatherer of my granddaughter, the gathering was at least proving out. She had a good eye, and a quick hand. We got six.

"Don't we want to get a few more, Grandpa?" Lara said.

And so we got two more, small ones, and I rigged a spinning rod without a reel, with line tied directly to the tip-top guide, to which I affixed a bright red-and-white bobber, then a length of level leader, then a smallish bait hook.

My friend Bill Kronenberg has a lovely spring-fed pond, an acre or so, filled with outsized trout, plump bullheads, and far too many bluegill. The latter were always ravenous. Perfect.

There is a photograph of us, taken recently — one old man, as big as a house, on a wooden dock, and a skinny little girl in a long pink cotton dress and sneakers and a floppy white hat. She is carrying a gigantic creel over her shoulder and holding a long rod from which dangles, unceremoniously, a pancake-sized bluegill, her first. The old man has his arm around her waist so that she will not fall in. The girl is serious about her first bluegill.

Lara's grandmother, who took the photograph, later reported that I had clearly made a convert, though I remember reflecting soberly that even our six bluegill — and all the chattering about them afterward — did not an angler make.

But the photo does give reason for hope. *(October 27, 2002)*

SALTWATERS

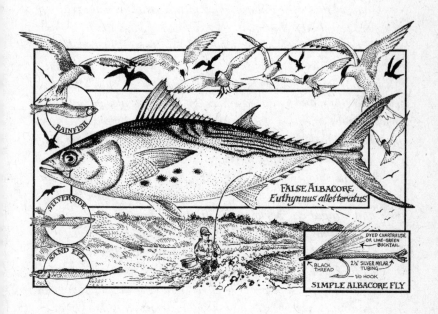

RAINFISH

SILVERSIDE

SAND EEL

FALSE ALBACORE
Euthynnus alletteratus

DYED CHARTREUSE
OR LIME-GREEN
BUCKTAIL

BLACK
THREAD

2½" SILVER MYLAR
TUBING

1/0 HOOK

SIMPLE ALBACORE FLY

Unlike fishing for trout and salmon, where the fundamental techniques have stayed essentially the same for the better part of a century, angling in saltwater — particularly for inshore species — has evolved in quantum leaps in just the past fifteen years. In many ways, "Outdoors" has chronicled this short history, which includes the incredible return of the striped bass to the Northeast, the explosion of saltwater fly-fishing, and the metamorphosis of the false albacore from "trash fish" into movie-star status.

Having said that, it would be remiss not to point out that Nelson Bryant has fly-fished for stripers since the 1940s. He also pursued false albacore (not to mention bluefish and bonito) with a fly rod decades before it became fashionable, using tackle that would make today's gearhead fly-rodders shudder in their Gore-Tex.

Saltwater anglers have transformed themselves, too. Oilskins and canvas waders have given way to breathable everything. Handheld GPS units and dreaded cell phones have infiltrated beaches and boats. Of course, the tackle industry has responded in kind to this lust for all things technical. Not too long ago, Orvis carried exactly one saltwater fly line called just that: Saltwater Fly Line. Now there is an ungodly array to choose from, tapered for every conceivable species and condition.

Thankfully, the buzz of high-tech tackle gets lost quickly in the lonely places where saltwater fish are found, places of awesome power such as a November surf whipped by a nor'easter, or a rushing tide rip where forty-pound bass prowl under the darkness of a new moon.

CASTING INTO THE PAST
FOR STRIPED BASS HEAVEN

By C. J. Chivers

THE BOULDERS THAT loom in the shallows of Point Judith, Rhode Island, are debris from the last ice age, having been scoured off the underlying stone some 12,000 years ago, only to be scattered, like so much construction rubble, when the ice retreated from the mouth of Narragansett Bay.

Each summer, schools of striped bass gather in the heavy waves that wash over these rocks, completing migration routes they have traveled since glaciers changed their world. They are mature, savvy predators. Some are longer than a man's leg.

Sometime in the darkness on a recent Friday night, my father stood in a small boat that rose and fell just outside the point's crashing surf. His rod was slumped over and bouncing. He was fighting the sixth or seventh fish to come to the gunnel during a busy, moonless hour.

Captain Joe Pagano shined a light into the blackness, illuminating the outline of a pale brute with flared gills and thrashing head. He lifted the dripping bass and worked out the hook. A twenty-one-pounder.

As fishermen go, my father is extraordinarily finicky. Let it be known that James Chivers doesn't want big fish. He doesn't want little fish. He wants succulent keepers precisely

117

at legal size, which in Rhode Island is twenty-nine inches. This fish was about thirty-nine inches long. No good. Pagano turned it back.

The recovery of striped bass stocks during the 1990s has invigorated all manner of inshore fishing methods. Pagano, a skipper for twenty-one years, has resurrected the most elemental: the inshore eel-casting trip. Like the charter captains of yesteryear, Pagano weaves a twenty-three-foot boat in and out of the surf's edge, holding the hull tight to submerged stones and ledges, hazarding the turbulent shallows where bass roam at night. His work at the helm gives fishermen access to a rich intermediate zone, a belt of water beyond the range of shore fishermen and beyond the daring of most people in boats.

He describes it like this: "I've already hit all the rocks. So I know where they are."

Eel-casting at night is all fundamentals. You take a live eel, a foot or more long, and slide a stout hook through its head. Pagano moves the boat in position while you whisk long casts toward small targets. The eels plop down and you reel them back slowly, presenting them as easy victims for the big, migratory fish that lie in ambush by the boulders.

When a fish hits a foot-long eel, usually it's a big fish, and usually it smashes the bait. If you prefer twenty-nine-inchers, you might have to wait.

Why would anyone prefer twenty-nine-inchers? The truth is this: my father is an unconverted meat fisherman with his own exacting standards.

In 1955 he fished the tidewaters of Virginia's Rappahannock River. Back then, small bass, twenty- to twenty-two-inchers, filled acres of the river's wide surface, slashing at schools of bait under a wheeling sky of gulls. There were so many fish in 1955 that my father, then a teenager, did not have to bother giving casting directions to my grandfather, who had been blinded in a hunting accident nine years before.

Once they found the schools, anywhere they threw lures there were fish. Bass were everywhere. Even a blind man could catch them. My father is a shy man, and he holds his emotions close, but when he talks about the Rappahannock of 1955, his voice is tinged with joy.

He has seen his ideal, and he saw it young. And having acquired his taste for striped bass on the small, tender fish of the Rappahannock, he wants none of Point Judith's larger, tougher fish. All he wants, a few times each year, is a single twenty-nine-incher, the sweetest catch he can bring home without risking a state summons.

Out on the water with Pagano, the Point Judith bass were weak for eels. They came readily to the boat. One by one we turned them back: a thirteen-pounder (thirty-three inches), a seventeen-pounder (thirty-six inches), and five clones at twenty-one and twenty-two pounds (thirty-nine or forty inches). Finally the fishing slowed and we moved, heading north up the bay.

Shortly before 1:00 a.m., we eased up to a spot where a small contingent of submerged boulders could be picked out by ripples in the swells. The air was laced with the aroma of honeysuckle. Dad was still at work. He is sixty-one. His shoulders were stiff. His casts were more conservative, low on snap and vigor. But soon he hooked another large bass, which he fought halfway to the boat before it slipped the hook.

Quickly he heaved the eel back to the same spot and—wham!—was on again. The fish seemed lighter. And as it raced by the boat, its short, slender form was silhouetted by Pagano's light. Dad smiled. "Too small," I said, as it came out of the water.

Pagano produced a measuring tape. There it was: the twenty-nine-incher. The night's smallest bass, my father's perfect catch.

We stowed the tackle. Pagano throttled the engine into gear. A half hour later we were gliding over a salt pond's tranquil surface when a tangerine-colored moon rose up out of the Atlantic.

Big eels. Shallow water. Forty-five years from the Rappahannock. Fresh dinner on ice. *(July 4, 2000)*

A GLORIOUS SHOW OF STRIPED
BASS WITHOUT A CATCH

By Nick Lyons

ORT SAID, POSITIVELY, ABSOLUTELY, "There is no bait in the surf at Amagansett, and no fish." So, with the bones in my right hip feeling as though someone had rasped away all of the cartilage, I wasn't much up for fishing. I had slipped in May, gone under in a river, smacked my head on a stone. Now it was August and I would get a titanium hip in three weeks.

It would be a quiet family jaunt is all, son-in-law driving, granddaughter beside me in the backseat singing, no fly rods to complicate my life. Mort said there were no fish in the surf, and Mort is an honorable and wise friend who is never wrong on matters piscatorial.

On the first morning, at the gentleman's hour of eleven, I limped to the beach and surveyed the vast, gray ocean. The tide was out, the white breakers were a hundred yards offshore. A few terns flew swiftly overhead, head and beak slanted down, searching; three seagulls foraged what the sea had left.

I dug my cane deeply into the wet sand, like Ahab with his wooden leg, and saw a hundred yards to my left a few birds clustered in the sky. Ah, birds. To an angler anywhere they are icons and emblems, harbingers of drama, so I hobbled north and saw that they were dipping, darting, plunging hard into the sea. I had seen this before, but never at midday. There had to be a little bait in the water was all, perhaps a few two-pound bluefish among it.

In fact, the low tide, the particular cross-movements of the waves, had built a vast trough or wash, some three football fields long, one wide, and when I got close enough I could see that there were really forty birds, careening and plunging, making my old heart flutter, and that some of the birds came out of the sea looking like aerial Fu Manchus, with a curled mustache hanging from either side of their beaks, and on the beach there were sand eels flopping, four or five inches long, so that was what all the fuss was about, sand eels.

At first I thought the two forms in the foam and vying currents, moving parallel to the shore, were skin divers. Then I thought they might be seals. Were there seals in Amagansett? Or walruses? They kept moving irregularly back and forth, fifty feet in from the breakers, their great bodies bulging the surface at times, then disappearing, then protruding above it, now closer to the shore, now no more than eighty feet from me — and I was twenty feet back from where the water reached. Wading in the suds, I could reach whatever was out there with merely a modest fly cast.

Striped bass. That's what was out there. Two, possibly three gigantic stripers, perhaps fifty pounds, maybe sixty, as happy as tarpon eating Cuban sardines, in no hurry whatsoever. They and some of the smaller fish I now saw — stripers, not bluefish — had herded the sand eels in against the shore and were systematically gorging on them.

It was a glorious sight — once in a lifetime: bull or cow stripers, perhaps world records, within casting distance, glutting on sand eels, oblivious to all else, vulnerable, a little like me when there's a table full of strawberry shortcake.

I happen to own fifty-three of the finest sand-eel imitations made. Lou Tabory had given me a sample many years ago, on a long shank hook with silver body, short red tag, long green spade hackles — and I had wisely had a fine tier in Maine make me a lifetime supply. I had caught blues and stripers on them and knew with absolute certainty that they would take fish in this trough. It was comforting to know that they were safe in my fish closet, in New York City.

For a moment I thought wildly about gimp-hopping back to the room, corralling my son-in-law into driving me to town, buying a whole new outfit, rushing back. No. Even a dumb-bell knew that would take at least a half hour, and this freak show of nature would be over in twenty minutes. Maybe I should call Mort on a cell phone; he lived nearby. But I didn't have his number and I didn't have a cell phone. So I sat down on the bench of sand that marked high tide and watched, eyes widening, then widening more.

A full two hours later the trough finally began to fill, the breakers came closer to shore, the birds drifted away, and the curtain came down on this diabolical show.

You must know that I'm dumb, but not dumb enough to have missed yet another fishing lesson that day.

You know I'll always harbor a touch of hope amid the well-earned doubts of an old fisherman.

You know I'll never go anywhere, ever, without a fly rod.

You know where Mort can go. *(August 13, 2000)*

BLITZES ARE THE GREAT HATCHES
OF THE SEA FOR ANGLERS

By John Waldman

IF THERE IS safety in numbers, you wouldn't know it in a blitz.

Blitzes are to saltwater gamefishing what the most exalted hatches are to trout fishing, and more. Panicked bait fish — anchovies, menhaden, sand eels, and pilchards — are the marine analogues to salmon flies on the Madison River, Green Drakes on the Delaware, and stoneflies on the Snake. But despite the bravura shown by insect-mad trout, their seeming abandon is relative only to their famous caution. No matter what the intensity of the hatch, there remains an aura of delicateness to the scene. Yes, both a great hatch and a blitz are to be enjoyed for their often fleeting moments of angling nirvana, but the blitz is also to be appreciated as nature at its most naked — a muscular combustion of predator and prey.

Place experienced trout anglers at a blitz and they may feel out of their league, or even overwhelmed. A friend calmly brought a couple of freshwater fly-fishermen by boat to the edge of a mob of bluefish ripping through menhaden. Not only were his guests afraid to cast into what one called "the white wall of death" — they were fearful for their lives.

Short for *Blitzkrieg*, or "lightning war" in German, the blitz may be found in any seas where gamefish seek baitfish; in the United Kingdom a blitz is called a "munch-up," in Australia, a "boil-up," and everywhere a feeding frenzy. The circumstances of each blitz vary, but at its essence a school of predators attacks a shoal of smaller prey. In deeper water the assault may come from below, pinning the victims against the surface where leaping is their only recourse. In the shallows, death arrives sideways with the bait fish driven against and even upon the shore.

Some species are famous for blitzing. Bluefish are consummate practitioners; even as baby "snapper" blues, they terrorize silversides in quiet harbors with all the fury of ocean-run adults, just on a miniaturized scale. The dentally endowed bluefish tear into bait-fish schools, literally cutting them down to size and leaving heads and tails drifting about, to be consumed as the quarry retreat. Striped bass are not less reticent, but lacking cutting teeth, they swallow their prey whole.

Truly exceptional blitzes have reached legendary status, such as the 1981 "Columbus Day Blitz" on Martha's Vineyard. In the middle of the Vineyard's annual striper derby, two schools of heavyweight stripers and some outsized bluefish reinforcements corralled menhaden against the beach. Eventually the schools merged — like two low-pressure systems — producing a perfect storm of a blitz with twenty to thirty linesiders charging the bait fish at once. Hundreds of bass weighing thirty to fifty pounds and more were landed. Word spread throughout the island, with anglers leaving jobs and appointments to rush to the scene. One truck was so laden with fish that its tires were flattened to the rims.

Some fishes are unlikely blitzers. Whiting, a slim relative of the codfish, is usually found on deep offshore banks. But while seeking stripers one spring on a Long Island beach, I learned that whiting had been blitzing daily at dusk. I waited, and just as the sun edged below the horizon, the first break appeared. Soon the shallows teemed with whiting launching themselves off the bottom to seize sand eels, with dozens of the predators in the air at once. And just as sea lore has it, unaccustomed to this feeding mode, several whiting drove themselves upon the sand in mad pursuit. Hence the name "frostfish" for a species that in times of greater abundance could sometimes be gathered, already frozen, simply by walking winter shores.

In autumn, I enjoy scanning the surf for blitzes by driving from lookout to lookout. Once, when my young son Steve was along, I drove away from a spot, saying, "There's nothing here." Steve, quite reasonably, asked, "But, Dad, how do you know? Fish live *underwater*." The boy had a point. But to an angler searching for fish, the sea is immense and too often appears vacant, whereas a blitz is usually a promise fulfilled. But first you must find one.

Although blitzes may be riotous up close, there are subtleties to detecting them from afar. Practiced eyes may spot the commotion from a distance, but often there is an easier way: watch the birds. Seabirds almost always capitalize on the ensuing confusion, plucking prey fish from above while providing aerial markers for anglers who know to look for "birds working." Fish and bird may even vie for the same prey; a friend watched as a British sea bass and a gull each hung on to an end of a sand eel. Perhaps because gravity was in its favor, the bass prevailed.

When birds are working, it's worthwhile to study them closely. Gulls are surefire signals — heavy and awkward, more scavenger than predator, they capitalize on the carnage. But terns, tiny and gracile, are so adept at seizing baitfish underwater that a flock can simulate a blitz with nary a gamefish present. When terns dart above a true blitz, but don't dare to submerge, it signals potentially dangerous bluefish below. And gannets indicate big baitfish, usually sea-herring, which in the Northeast draw great stripers in late autumn.

But blitzes can also happen at night, minus the birds. Telltale signs are the smacking noises feeding stripers make; another is a sound like rain as baitfish leap and fall back into the sea. When intense blitzes occur, it's possible in daylight to see fine oil slicks, regions where the water is flattened by surface tension from the fats released from the chopped bodies. Even more esoteric is to sniff for them — there may be a faint cucumber or melon odor surrounding bluefish blitzes. What causes this remains unproven, but the leading theory is that it is the smell of plankton emanating from the baitfishes' ruptured stomachs.

Part of the excitement of a blitz is its sheer dynamism. Both a great hatch and a blitz may end suddenly, but while it lasts, the trout enjoying a hatch aren't going anywhere. And when it's over, the fish simply drop to the bottom of the pool to digest their feast. But although some blitzes stay put for an hour or more, many migrate at high speed or leap from spot to spot as predators and prey regroup after each encounter, like fighters after the bell in a boxing match.

Once in a while, blitzes occur on so grand a scale — nature's annual cycle reaching a crescendo — that the scene mirrors Steinbeck's description of the Sea of Cortez as "ferocious with life." One memorable November morning, striper schools stretched before me for miles down the center of Long Island Sound; for every fish showing, there were dozens below. White flapping wings filled the air and the songs of gulls *a capella* played in my ears while the surface boiled as if being heated from a fire below. Time and again my offering was attacked before I could engage the reel, providing a swift and sweet balance to many the fishless trip.

But perhaps we should temper our excitement over blitzes by recognizing the harsh reality of the doomed baitfish. A blitz is really the sum of countless individual encounters among gamefish, baitfish, and, often, birds. A friend witnessed this phenomenon in its purest, most distilled form. Looking out from his vessel at sea, he saw a lone flying fish bounding toward the sunset. Each time it arced through the air a gannet dove at it; whenever it touched down, a dolphinfish boiled behind it. The chase continued so far into the distance that he never saw who won, but the identity of the loser is not in question. *(November 23, 2003)*

THE SPECIAL TESTS OF
PLAYING FISHING GUIDE

By Nelson Bryant

M ARTHA'S VINEYARD, MASS. — A generous degree of confidence is required to invite friends to angle in your home waters, particularly if you are — rightly or wrongly — regarded as something of an expert.

There is always the possibility during the few days you have decided to play host that the fish you are seeking will not be around or that the weather will be unfavorable.

Every professional fishing guide or charter boat skipper faces this all season long, but they — though displeased by failure — eventually acquire a healthy degree of emotional detachment. It's a day's work in which you do the best you can.

When guiding friends on an informal basis, you also get to fish. With a paying client this is usually taboo, and when the client fails to hook up, there is always the thought that things would be different were the rod in your hands.

With friends, there is a fair chance — a drawback, if you worry about tarnishing your image — that they will do better than you. Newcomers to your area, unfettered by decades of local angling expertise, try outlandish flies or lures in dubious locations and sometimes catch fish while you are sitting on a rock smoking your pipe, waiting for them to heed your advice and move on.

Last winter I told a friend, Willard Weeks of Amherst,

Massachusetts, that the shore fly-fishing for striped bass on Martha's Vineyard Island is superlative in June, and before the phone conversation ended, we had made plans for him and his wife, Barbara, to visit Ruth and me in June. Shortly before his arrival, Will called to say that he had injured his knee and was unable to do much walking.

This was a setback. I had planned to spend most of our time fishing a section of Lobsterville Beach known as Dogfish Bar. Because of the unusually wet spring, the dirt road to that location had been flooded for more than a month and was impassable. The spot could be reached by a half-hour hike along the beach in waders, but that was out of the question for my guest.

❖   ❖   ❖

On the afternoon he arrived, Will asked if I would give his wife a short lesson in fly-casting. I discovered that she could get out a short line, thirty feet or so. That would suffice, I told her, because bass often come to within a rod's length of shore at night, when most of the fly-fishing for bass on the Vineyard is done.

Will's bad knee and Barbara's short casts notwithstanding, we caught fish on each of the three nights we went out. On the first night the bass were breaking a few feet from shore, and Barbara soon had her first fly-rod stripers.

On another evening, after taking half a dozen small bass, Will wondered aloud about the chances of catching a "keeper" — in Massachusetts, the recreational limit is one bass a day, twenty-eight or more inches long — to take home with him. I told him that that wasn't likely because all the fish in front of us seemed to be small.

A few minutes later, while releasing yet another bass about twenty-two inches long, Will allowed his fly to dangle in the water from his rod tip. There was a big swirl as a fish took it, and ten minutes later he had his keeper, a striper well over the minimum length limit. So much for a local expert's predictions. On that night he also caught twice as many fish as his guide did.

A day before the Weekses showed up, I had gone fishing for stripers one evening with Harold "Buster" Welch, of Winnipeg, Manitoba, who was visiting the Vineyard with his family. Buster had written me earlier in the year asking about the best times and locations for fly-fishing the island's bass. He immediately began catching fish at Lobsterville Beach, including one keeper, a fillet of which he presented to Ruth and me.

Buster really didn't need my input. An energetic, enterprising, and engaging fellow, he had, by inquiring locally and consulting maps, pinpointed all the likely spots and was taking fish wherever he went.

The fillet he gave me was much appreciated because none of the sixty or seventy bass I had caught up to that time had been large enough to keep. Equally appreciated was his gift of two swatches of polar-bear hair for tying flies, a rare material that I had never possessed before.

The road to Dogfish Bar dried out a few days after the Weekses left, and while I was out there one night, still trying to get my first keeper, a young fly-fisherman came up to me in the dark and introduced himself. He was Dave Radcliffe of Northampton, Massachusetts, whom I had taken fishing at Lobsterville nearly a decade before.

Dave and I caught a few small bass in the next two hours, and at midnight I called it quits, offering the opinion that no big fish were going to show. Dave stuck it out, and shortly before dawn caught four stripers well over the legal limit, keeping one to give to me.

It occurred to me I might be able to keep bass in the

freezer by wandering the beaches at night, telling friends I encountered that I was unable to catch big fish.

Several days later I was back at Dogfish alone, resolved to end the no-keeper syndrome. In the first two hours after sunset I caught twenty-four bass, and two of them were only an inch or two short of the legal limit. Bigger bass had to be out there. Perhaps they wanted something different. I thought of the fly I had tied, using, among other things, a couple of dozen long strands of polar-bear hair. How fitting, I thought, to catch my first keeper of the season by making use of Buster Welch's gift.

On my second cast with that fly, a heavy fish hit and a minute or so later was deep into the backing, more than 150 yards offshore. It was going with the swift-running, falling tide and five minutes went by before I got it turned and headed my way.

I relaxed. I had broken the jinx, and skill and perseverance were being rewarded. The rest was routine and I was pleased that I'd had the foresight before I left home to rig an outside light over my cleaning table.

It was then that the hook pulled free. *(July 27, 1997)*

A STEALTHY PURSUIT
OF THE STRIPED BASS

By Peter Kaminsky

MONTAUK, N.Y. — What is so rare as a day in June (with apologies to the poet James Russell Lowell)?

A striped bass in skinny water on a day in June.

At 7:30 a.m., there were the barest wisps of clouds in an otherwise unbroken blue vault. As we pulled out of the marina, instead of making for the mouth of Three Mile Harbor, Paul Dixon hesitated for a moment and turned left.

He picked up his pole, scanned the water, and said, "This is the prettiest flat. There's no boat traffic stirring up the fish yet, so let's give it a try."

Every angler knows that to get good fishing you have to drive far, paddle far, walk far. It is part of the deal. So, I held out no hope for this maneuver and stared dreamily into the middle distance, munching on my breakfast — a Hershey bar with almonds — when Paul, sotto voce, commanded, "Nice fish, thirty feet, three o'clock."

I sent a backcast to a green ghost of a fish cruising along the line where the white, sandy shoal turned to a ribbon of sea grass, its dark fringe not grass at all, but schools of wriggling sand eels that were no longer than your finger.

"You landed in back of him," said Paul, my guide and

friend. As he admonished me, the fish turned obligingly, opened its mouth, wide and white, and engulfed my fly. It streaked across the flat and I let it run until it tired: a thirty-incher, an auspicious start.

At this time of year the striped bass, recently arrived at their summer feeding grounds from their winter homes in Chesapeake Bay and the Delaware and Hudson Rivers, are hungry and eminently fishable with a fly in the clear tidal flats. Seeing a striped bass, approaching it without alarming it, getting one or two casts off before the fish is alerted — an experience that combines the grace of fly-fishing with the stealth of stalking a deer in a forest.

Once outside the harbor, we poled the flats at either side of the entrance. We saw fish materialize out of the depths — seen for just a second, like familiar faces on the periphery of a dream. The incoming tide, nearly a flood, made it hard to reach the fish before they saw us. By the time the fly could sink to their level, they were onto our game. There were lots of big fish, but we could do no more than window-shop.

Paul decided to run west, where the tide was less advanced. The wind dropped, the sun rose, and I thought that finally I had prime conditions. But with absolutely no chop on the water, the glare made it hard to see. Paul spotted some fish, but I had trouble seeing them. It was not until I saw one on another backcast that I truly wired into the flats game.

From forty feet the fly, a Clouser with a slim sand-eel silhouette, landed in front of three fish. One of them turned.

"Leave it," Paul said. "Now strip, strip." The fish followed. "Leave it." The fish came to the fly. "Now tease him hard, strip, strip, strip, and leave it."

The striped bass, its predatory instincts challenged, pounced on the fly before it could escape. It was not a great fish, but decent.

We poled the flat for miles. The dark shadows, which had

been indistinguishable, now looked more like fish or grass or rocks. Fish move, grass and rocks do not. The bait, like clouds moving across the sky, drifted past us, tens of thousands of shimmering sand eels. On the shore the plovers piped and squeaked and squawked. We moved into a school of fifty bass, then another, then another. Where to cast first? The number of opportunities stymied me and left me flailing. I lighted a cigar and sat down in the hot, still air. I felt light-headed.

❖ ❖ ❖

Paul broke into my reverie in a low, conspiratorial tone. "All right, at five-thirty, eighty feet, coming toward us. I am going to turn the boat to give you a forehand shot."

He pivoted the boat on his push pole. "When you think you have it, take it," he said. "Lead him."

I pulled on my double haul, and cast into the shallow water, where three shapes moved parallel to the shore. One of them turned. I stripped. He followed. I stopped. He charged. I stripped and stopped two more times and he was on my fly like a blitzing linebacker.

"Good fish. Don't try to stop him," Paul counseled.

The bass ran around in a circle. I had to pass my rod around Paul's legs as I followed his course. After a splendid fight, a fourteen-pound bass came to my hand. I unhooked him and watched him melt back onto the flat: alive and present one second, gone the next.

Now is the high tide of the year, Lowell wrote. Fish it while you can. *(June 17, 2001)*

TESTING A HYPOTHESIS ON
TIME AND RIVER FISHING

By James Gorman

PIERMONT, N.Y. — Each spring, striped bass migrate up the Hudson River in the millions. I can see the Hudson in the distance from my house, and although I can't actually see the fish, I can imagine a living wave rippling north to spawn and soak up PCBs.

Eight years ago my son and I caught a thirty-inch striper off the mile-long pier, an old railroad spur (the tracks are long gone) that juts into the Hudson in Piermont, New York. The minimum length in the river is eighteen inches, and small school bass are common around the pier, so that was a good fish.

Since then the fishing has really slowed down — for us, anyway. I had a small boat for a few years, but always seemed to get the tide wrong. The rule about the tides, as I understand it, is that you should be fishing the one you're not. Since health advisories suggest that, because of PCBs in the river, I should eat no more than one striper a month, and my children none at all, I could look on bad luck as a healthy lifestyle. But I don't.

Time and tide are related, of course. It is well known that you can only catch fish yesterday. You can prove this law of nature by talking to any fisherman, anywhere. He will always say, "You should have been here yesterday." Unfortunately, whenever I fish, it's always today.

This year, however, I found a wrinkle in time. I walked the pier on a couple of days after the season started on March 16 (the season for keeping fish, though the actual fishing goes on year-round) and heard of a few fish being caught. Then my neighbors told me, on Monday, that on Sunday everyone was catching stripers on the pier.

On a weekday afternoon I took my equipment, including a folding chair and a deli lunch, and drove out to the end of the pier (automobile permits are free for residents, but can cost up to $175 a year for nonresidents). I found a fairly secluded spot and baited two lines with bloodworms. They are aptly named, and putting them on a hook is something like an Aztec ritual sacrifice. I cast out the baited rigs and sat down in my folding chair to contemplate the differences between still fishing and fly-fishing.

For one thing, with fly-fishing you don't get worm blood on your hands, so lunch is a more pleasant experience. Another difference is that despite its vaguely mystical aura, fly-fishing is a lot like work. I'm a frenetic fly-fisherman. I wade up and down rivers and streams, looking for good spots, changing flies, usually falling and breaking some piece of equipment. Or I stand still and work myself into a frenzy about what fly I should use. I love fly-fishing, but it has never given me a moment's peace.

Bait-fishing is the true path to serenity. When you bait up a hook with a gob of bloodworms and cast it out into the river, there is nothing to do but wait. You can doze, or check your bait occasionally, or your pulse, if you're not sure you're still alive. You can move spots if you like, but the essence of still fishing is being still.

I sat, I watched the river and the gulls. I felt the wind. I was overtaken by the slow and uncooperative rhythms of nature. Time passes. Fish bite. Or not. I did not catch fish. I did, however, achieve enlightenment, so the day wasn't a total bust.

My great insight — the moment of truth — was when I remembered that my grandmother used to say, "Today is the tomorrow you worried about yesterday." Perhaps, I thought, there was a fishing corollary, as jumbled, irrational, and confusing as the original. What if tomorrow was the yesterday the lucky fishermen were always telling me about?

The next morning I tested my hypothesis. I drove out to a spot on the north side of the pier and stopped to talk to some of the regulars, Jimmy Mulligan, Peter Catanese, and John Francesconi, known to his friends as the Michael Jordan of the Hudson.

On the pier, most of the regulars are retired. A number of them are involved with the New Jersey chapter of the Hudson River Fisherman's Association. They not only fish, they also tag bass to track their movements, lobby for access to the river, and release almost all of the fish they catch.

I was trying to get the regulars to tell me how to catch fish. They wanted to impress on me how the fishing regulations should change: a bigger minimum size for keeping bass, and a rule requiring that all females with roe be released.

Eventually I extracted some useful information, and set up at a recommended spot, facing the incoming tide as it was nearing its high point. This time I put really big, bloody gobs of worms on the hook. (O Quetzalcoatl, hear my prayer.) The sky started to darken, the wind picked up, and the fish started to hit. For the next hour or so, they kept biting. The first fish I pulled in was probably about eighteen inches. Two men next to me started catching fish as well. Then the wind picked up even more and a light rain started and I heard someone shout, "They're all over the place."

I caught five fish, most short, and kept one that was nineteen inches. Once I had the fish I was going to eat, I stopped.

By then the rain was coming down. I took the striper home, filleted and sautéed it, and had my ritual spring dinner, most likely the only striper I'll kill all year.

I went to sleep that night satisfied, and the next morning I woke up with a smile, My plan had worked. Finally, I had been there yesterday. *(April 14, 2002)*

PLAYING HIDE-AND-SEEK
WITH THE MONSTER BLUEFISH

By Pete Bodo

East Hampton, N.Y. — By the time the captain, David Blinken, turned the stubby nose of his seventeen-foot flats skiff into the sheltered cove where we hoped to fish, it was clear that if a day can be described in psychiatric terms, this one was manic-depressive. Just hours earlier, under bright and balmy June skies, Blinken had been poling me and the photographer Richard Franklin along the open, shallow flats of Napeague Bay as we made delicate presentations with small, feathery flies to visible striped bass in the six- to ten-pound class.

The fish mostly ate the flies. We mostly landed and released the fish. The sun warmed our necks and we exchanged dumb jokes and high fives with childlike gusto.

But by noon a cold front rolled in, chilly rain hissed and spat at us, and, because ours was a small, open craft, Blinken felt obliged to tune his radio to the National Oceanic and Atmospheric Administration broadcast. Whereupon a creepy, digitalized voice coldly warned us that the wind might gust to forty miles per hour.

Thus we were relieved to beat it into Napeague, a quiescent place tucked into the lee of all the turbulence, where the water was olive but flat; where the clouds were mere stains in a uniformly gray sky; where a large white egret stood out conspicuously amid the luminous and pale green marsh grasses along the shore. And where, each of us was thinking without saying, we might hang a truly big fish. For something about ominous skies and big weather and secret places almost always whispers "Big Fish."

"Look at the shake in the water, two o'clock, about 150 yards out," Blinken said from the poling platform, as he slid the skiff along, just a few feet from shore. "That's a school of fish. A big school. And they're big fish."

❖ ❖ ❖

I stood on the bow of the skiff, waiting for the fish to break water within range, aware of the rain beating a tattoo on the shoulders of my jacket. Blinken had insisted on switching to a larger, heavier fly now that we were no longer fishing the thin, clear water. It could not have been more than four feet deep where we were anchored, but it might just as well have been twenty fathoms. The surface was dark and impenetrable.

"There," Blinken called out. We all simultaneously saw the small explosions of water, the sucking boils and sharp swirls made by feeding fish. "Give me a shot of about fifty feet, eleven o'clock."

I had stripped back two feet of line after making my cast when a fish took the fly decisively. The slack line coiled around my feet, slapped against the deck, and whistled out of the guides as I tried, unsuccessfully, to raise the rod against the weight of the fish. Then the powerful fish broke water, sending a spume of water high in the air and landing back on its side with an audible smack.

"It's a bluefish," Blinken cried. "It's a giant blue."

"Are you sure?" I asked, incredulous.

Although stripers and, in the fall, false albacore are the preferred quarry for most Northeastern inshore fly-fishers, I had for a long time harbored a secret desire to catch a monster bluefish—one of those ferocious, ten-pound-plus fish that are commonly called Gorilla Blues.

As a boy, I had caught eight-inch-long, juvenile "snapper" blues in Barnegat Bay, and had marveled at the uncommon strength and speed and the precocious attack instinct within their slender, silver bodies. Over the years I landed plenty of "cocktail" and "tailor" and "chopper" blues—this is a fish with more nicknames than menacing qualities—respectively denoting fish of roughly two, five, and eight pounds, and admired the ferocity with which they blitzed and decimated hapless baitfish until the sea ran red.

There is no more feckless and relentless a predator, wet or dry, than the common bluefish. Among other survival advantages, it can increase or decrease the amount of gas in its swim bladder faster than any other fish, allowing it to change depth more quickly.

Still, the giant blues are fish of the black water, generally disinclined to spend much time in the shallows. I had come across an exception, and I had my hands full.

Once again, the giant bluefish beat the surface to a froth with its thrashing, and then it began to swim determined, powerful circles around the boat, drawing line from the grudging reel. We could see its thick body, instinctively turned to offer the most resistance against the rod, and even a great, large eye. Eventually it would tire, and the truth is that in the battle between man and fish, man almost always wins.

"Got him," Blinken said as he clamped the steel Boga Grip on the lower jaw of the big blue. He needed both hands to haul the fish into the boat. It was green on top and along the spine, fading to blue and silver on its flanks. When Blinken turned the fish, iridescent yellow and pink and blue tones appeared.

❖ ❖ ❖

A stout but streamlined body enables the blue to produce tremendous bursts of speed, but the most distinguishing feature of this fish was the prominent lower jaw, lined with a single row of conical teeth. The teeth of the bluefish are so sharp that instead of capturing and swallowing its prey, it often tears off and swallows chunks of it. Blues are so greedy and wasteful that when a marauding school attacks bait like menhaden, the fat, oil, and other liquids and body parts left by the carnage leave a conspicuous "bluefish slick," much like an oil spill.

The bluefish weighed a shade over twelve pounds. It lay on the floor of the boat, gasping. I reached toward it, but Blinken, alarmed, warned me to keep my fingers clear. I looked at its unblinking, baleful, amber eye before we released it. It was an awesome fish that commanded the same thing as most great predators and the next best thing to love: respect. *(July 8, 2001)*

AS YOU CAST, WATCH OUT
FOR LOW-FLYING PLANES

By Stephen Sautner

A 747 THUNDERED DOWN Kennedy Airport's southeastern runway, lumbering into the air just as Richard Reagan double-hauled seventy feet of fly line into the calm waters of Jamaica Bay. The plane banked to the west; Reagan stripped his line twice, and promptly hooked into another striped bass.

In a city known for such oddball fishing locations as sewage outfalls, stagnant canals, and rotting piers, the deep hole next to JFK may be the strangest of all. Dredged in the 1940s to provide fill for the airport's runways, the forty-five-foot-deep depression literally swarms with striped bass, bluefish, and weakfish each spring. Throw in an unending procession of low-flying aircraft, not to mention tens of thousands of boisterous laughing gulls nesting nearby, and you have an experience as sublime as Times Square on New Year's Eve.

"This is sensory overload," yelled Reagan, trying to be heard over yet another jet, as he battled his fish. He eventually pressured the bass to the boat, where it was quickly scooped up by Captain John McMurray, a guide who has fished around JFK for the past ten years.

McMurray measured the fish at thirty inches, a lean spring-run striper that had probably spent the winter in the nearby

144

Hudson River. "We should see some bigger ones today," he said, releasing our third fish in half an hour.

After a few more casts, McMurray decided to motor us toward a shallow flat near a sedge island crowded with nesting gulls and terns. As we approached, a growing cacophony of ha-ha-haah-haahs, kyarrs, and kik-kik-kiks rose over the island, as clouds of calling birds swooped and dived above their nests. We drew closer when an odd popping sound echoed from the direction of the airport. "Cannons," McMurray explained. "They scare the gulls off the runway."

I started to ask whether he thought the cannon fire bothered the nesting birds, but a well-timed DC-10 drowned me out.

McMurray then cut the engine, allowing us to drift slowly onto the flat. We watched, rods at the ready, as the bottom steadily rose up to just a few feet from the surface. Clumps of seaweed and scattered clamshells could now be seen in the clear water.

Just as Reagan and I cast, McMurray yelled, "Oh my God, look," and pointed to dozens of large swirls no more than twenty feet off the bow of the boat. "We just spooked a school of big bass. There's twenty-pounders in there," he said, managing to get off a short cast. The line landed near one of the fleeing stripers, which immediately wheeled around and inhaled his fly.

"Got him," McMurray said with a grunt, jabbing the rod a few times to set the hook. The striper then realized its mistake and tore off, taking line in bursts while shaking its head. After a few shorter runs and dives for the bottom, a thirty-three-incher came to the boat with McMurray's bulky chartreuse streamer — called a J. Bay Giant — hanging in the scissors of its jaw.

The dropping tide slowly pulled us off the flat into deeper water, where a school of tightly packed mossbunker splashed along the surface. Beginning in April, these slab-sided plankton feeders crowd into backbays by the millions, where they are inevitably followed by everything from hungry ospreys to stripers.

Reagan and I both began casting to the sides of the school, letting our flies sink a foot or two before stripping them back to the boat. A brief respite between jets allowed us to listen to three chattering oystercatchers making their way overhead.

Midway through my next cast, the shadow of a bass appeared ghostlike behind my streamer. I continued stripping and the fish followed, now just a few yards from the boat. Finally, just before the fly literally ran out of water, the bass flashed silver and took it in a slow-motion gulp. The line tightened, then flew back through the guides of the rod and into the bay. A few minutes later, another ten-pounder was landed and released.

McMurray then spied a pod of diving terns and swirling bass that had pinned a school of smaller baitfish against a shoreline a few hundred yards away. We cranked up our lines and held on as he punched the throttle, sending us bouncing toward what was developing into a full-blown feeding frenzy.

He shut off the motor before reaching the fish, which were now boiling and slapping the surface. As soon as we drifted into range, Reagan and McMurray quickly shot streamers into the school. Hungry stripers grabbed the flies almost immediately.

Meanwhile, I had switched from a fly rod to a spinning rod rigged with a small wooden surface lure, and fired a cast just beyond the edge of the feeding fish. Two cranks of the handle, and a bass bulged up behind the lure. Another turn and the fish engulfed it, sending spray flying, and me shouting for joy.

With all three of us now hooked into stripers, Reagan and McMurray may have been yelling, too, but all I could see were their lips moving as another jumbo jet seemed to pass just over their bent rods before heading skyward. *(June 3, 2001)*

CAPE COD BEAUTY SEEN
EVEN BEFORE *MAYFLOWER*

BY MARGOT PAGE

THE MAP WAS HAND-DRAWN by the French explorer Champlain himself and dated 1605, predating the *Mayflower*'s Cape Cod landing by fifteen years.

The place he depicts is Nauset Harbor on the Atlantic shore of Cape Cod, a windswept landscape of ocean and dunes. Like spindly protective arms, two spits curving out from the harbor meet in a near touch, but not quite.

This entrance permits the rush and sweep of the daily tides into Nauset Harbor, which will become, in a century, a major New England port, and eventually, hundreds of years later, part of the protected national seashore.

Around the map's coast crowd the Nauset tribe's settlements: wooden fences enclose huts with smoke wafting above; these are, as translated from Champlain's map legend, "the houses and abodes of Indians who cultivate the soil." And there, on the sand dunes, is the carefully rendered image of a Nauset killing a French sailor, a visitor from Champlain's ship, the barque of the Sieur de Mons. Something about a kettle of fresh water.

I look at the rough-hewn map now in the warmth of my house, and remember how, only a few months ago but nearly four hundred years after Champlain debarked on this wild and sandy Cape Cod coastline, I was huddled with my fishing friends near the tailgate of a four-wheel-drive vehicle at the exact point where the Frenchman and his sailors stood.

To our backs, the lights of the houses encircling Nauset Harbor shone in the waning twilight. Behind them, the bright moon rose.

I had driven down from Vermont to visit my father, who lives on the Cape in Eastham, Massachusetts, bringing along my dog, Pete, my saltwater fishing gear, and some hostas and peonies to transplant into the garden. And now here I was, standing around with my fishing buddies in the steadily blowing salt wind, at Nauset Harbor, lighted by the stars, the quarter moon, and the faint light from the car's interior. We lurched away through the bumpy sand tracks over the very landscape labeled, simply, "Sea Shore" by Champlain.

When I returned to my father's dark house later that night, I laid my wet neoprenes across the weathered split-rail fence over which my mother's wild roses will crawl next summer, and then climbed the narrow, steep stairs to bed.

The salt wind was still rushing through my body. I fell asleep with the stars and the lights of Nauset Harbor twinkling in front of my eyelids; the wind and the waves had roared through me and filled me up. I could think of nothing else.

The next day, my artist fishing pal, Tony Stetzko, said he couldn't fish with me, but told me to go to Wellfleet Harbor, because "they were busting all over the place there yesterday." I hesitated because I had not yet fished saltwater by myself, even though my family has lived on the Cape for more than twenty years.

My male friends had always been my guides or my teachers, or Tom, my husband, had always been along. "But what if I actually catch a giant fish?" I whined to Tony in momentary panic. He sounded somewhat disgusted. "Just debarb the hook first," he said, and I was ashamed for being a wimp.

I packed my waders into the car and loaded up Pete, stopping at the Eastham Windmill deli to pick up a bag lunch. At Wellfleet Harbor, I parked at the end of the long, wide jetty. Next to me was another car, containing yet another fishing friend named Tony. We waited two hours for the tide to go out and bring the bait and stripers through the channel.

Meanwhile, two more fellows parked alongside. Out of the rearview mirror, I noticed that one of the new arrivals, finished with his briskly executed jumping jacks, was pushing his van very slowly around the vast parking lot — with his legs. He was a boxer in training, my friend Tony explained. Something about leg muscles.

The tide was finally right: we could see and hear the baitfish flipping up through the water's surface, chased by striper schoolies, the sound like raindrops, right off the jetty. I quickly rigged my fly rod and somewhat gingerly moved off on the rocks.

The other guys were spin-fishing, and I was aware, as the only woman and the only fly-fisher, that I was the object of some curiosity. But this surreptitious interest was friendly, even nurturing. Tony, already catching fish off the pier, generously yelled over for me to join him.

More bait erupted, and I landed some stripers, a couple in a row. Deciding to be bold, I moved over to the jetty again and out into the receding, waist-high water. I was unsure of the footing, but Tony told me the honey hole was off the submerged sandbar's point, beyond the tips of the marsh grass, and my greed prevailed over caution.

The bait again erupted, to my right, to my left, the patter of tiny bodies falling all around me. I forced myself to slow down my retrieve and, as a reward, felt the sudden heaviness of a take, then another, then another, then another striper on. Dark clouds moved in. The wind picked up.

Hours passed. I was alone and fishing Wellfleet. I was an explorer. I was drawing my own map. Something about being part of history. *(January 3, 1996)*

SEEKING REASSURANCE,

AND FINDING IT IN FISHING

By Pete Bodo

ONTAUK, N.Y.—We gurgled through the placid, opaque green water of Montauk Harbor, in the guide David Blinken's twenty-three-foot contender, as we had on so many other fall afternoons, debating green fly or white, floating or sinking line. As always, we were filled with childlike anticipation at the prospect of casting our flies to the striped bass and false albacore that were amassed in large schools in the shadow of the Montauk Point lighthouse, gorging on an infinite number of hapless baitfish.

As we motored past an enormous white clapboard building with a profusion of windows and red shutters, Blinken said, "Their big cutter pulled out on the afternoon of the eleventh. It hasn't been back since."

We fell silent, regarding the Coast Guard station at Montauk. It looked immaculate in the molten sunlight, and in front of it, the Stars and Stripes undulated gracefully in the gentle breeze. It was an unseasonably warm, glorious afternoon in a September that will always be remembered for the horrific events on the eleventh day of the month. And now, less than a week after the destruction of the World Trade Center, we were going fishing.

The breeze against my cheek felt cool and pleasant, the

salt air was bracing, and high overhead, a gull wheeled away from the sun, shrieking. In Manhattan, where workers with bulldozers continued trying to distinguish rubble from human remains, it had to be hot and ghastly.

I didn't know what thoughts my companions were entertaining, but I sensed that we were all thrilled to be going fishing; not far below the surface we all felt strange about it.

Soon we were beyond the jetty, just off Gin Beach, on whose tawny lap was collected the usual assortment of pickup trucks and sport utility vehicles and motor homes. They show up for the annual event known as the fall blitz of southward-migrating stripers, albies, and bluefish that congregate, along with the vast shoals of prey species, around Montauk Point. These anglers, mostly surf-casters, are basically a blue-collar crowd. They were as numerous as ever, but this year almost every vehicle flew a large United States flag.

"Hang on," Blinken shouted, as he pushed the throttles forward. "We've got a blitz. We've got albies."

When Blinken cut the engines moments later, we scrambled for our rods. Up ahead, almost within casting range, marauding false albacore were ripping into schools of bay anchovies. The swift albies, fish of eight to ten pounds, are as bright as steel and as sleek and maneuverable as warplanes. Panicked baitfish leaped and fell back into the water like rain, leaving large boils and silver spumes of spray. In their greed, the larger fish flew across the surface like torpedoes, or tumbled end-over-end in the gentle swells.

"There he is, he's on," called the photographer Richard Franklin, barely able to control his bucking rod. Arriving dockside barely an hour earlier, his first words had been something intended to comfort, something about peace. He felt the need to escape his preoccupation with the events of September 11, and shared his concern about the potential impact of those events on his twelve-year-old daughter, Julia.

I watched as Richard fought his fish. He looked determined; his jaw was set as if his very survival depended on landing this fish. He is a devoted fly-fisherman, a lifer. If this didn't provide him with some surcease, perhaps nothing could.

❖   ❖   ❖

The boat rolled violently, my head flew up, and I saw a disconcerting sight: a jumbo jet progressing through a thin, blue empty sky, nothing around it but air.

Nearby, the enormous littoral boulders, exploding waves, and bare, wind-swept cliffs would have amounted to a landscape of desolation, but for the presiding red-and-white lighthouse. I saw it with fresh eyes, understood the perfect marriage of function and symbolism in a stout conical building that continued to guide so many at sea and shore.

"Look at that," Blinken said.

Up ahead, nearly in the shadow of the lighthouse, the equivalent of an acre of water had become as white as the foamy head on a glass of draft beer. An untold number of fish were churning the water to a froth, and we soon made out the lavender-hued, striped sides and long, heavy bodies. They were bass, hundreds upon hundreds of them, engaged in a feeding spree so intense that an entire layer of fish was flopping around above the water, borne on the backs of other stripers, gasping, for lack of water.

We fell silent at this surreal, profligate display. The school of fish was so dense that the stripers thump, thump, thumped against the boat, oblivious of its presence, as we slowly drifted through the school. We didn't dare cast and retrieve our flies, knowing we would foul-hook a fish immediately by doing so. All we had to do was flip the fly over the edge of the boat, and immediately a bass between six and twenty pounds would take it.

Long after the blitz ended and the fish sounded, we remained preoccupied by what we had seen. On a day when people continue to need comfort and reassurance, the fertility of the sea had provided it for us. *(September 30, 2001)*

A FAMILIAR OLD POND

STILL BRINGS SURPRISES

By Nelson Bryant

WEST TISBURY, MASS. — In late October and early November, my grandson Jesse Child and I went after the young bluefish, or snappers, that had been trapped in Tisbury Great Pond when its opening to the ocean closed in early August. On our first trip we finally found them on a shallow flat against the barrier beach on the pond's west end. They were small, about eight inches long.

Bluefish are ocean spawners. Some spawn in late spring or early summer offshore, far south of New England, others move north and begin their procreative endeavors several weeks later. The fish we caught that day were clearly the offspring of the late spawners.

We kept a dozen of them to pan-fry for supper, and the results were so pleasing that we decided to try again. We had also been titillated by Jesse's capture of a fish much more common in southern waters, a species of jack crevalle known as the blue runner. The blue runner and the snappers would have departed for points offshore and south weeks before, had not the pond been closed.

Perhaps, we reasoned, there might be other summer visitors that had been similarly detained. We already knew that striped bass were among them.

Tucked behind a narrow barrier beach that separates it from the Atlantic, Tisbury Great Pond on Martha's Vineyard Island is many things to many people.

In summer, canoeists use it, and the bright sails of Sunfish and other small craft crisscross its surface. In fall and winter, commercial oystermen are at work, and waterfowlers huddle in its coves and marshes waiting for mallards, bluebills, teal, black ducks, and Canada geese.

The pond has permanent populations of blue-claw crabs, silverside minnows, mummichogs, shrimp, white perch, and eels. Spawning alewives visit it in spring, and a few brook trout may be found in the coves fed by its two major streams, Mill Brook and Tiasquam River.

The pond — if one discounts the major coves on its east shore — is about two miles long and three-quarters of a mile wide, and is opened to the ocean two or three times each year by man, when rain and its feeder brooks have filled it to the brim. Eventually it is closed by onshore storms and shifting sands. In years past, gangs of men and boys with shovels cut through the beach. Today a bulldozer does the job.

The most important reason for these periodic openings is to maintain the proper salinity for the pond's oysters, soft-shelled clams, and crabs. The torrent of relatively warm brackish water, laden with forage fish and crabs, pouring into the ocean on the falling tides, attracts striped bass and bluefish in late spring, summer, and fall. The snapper blues that Jesse and I caught had gone into the pond to feed on baitfish and to escape the predation of larger fish, including their own kind.

Bluefish and stripers of all ages are sometimes trapped in the pond for much of the winter. I recall one occasion in late November when, while setting out a dozen duck decoys in one of the pond's major coves, I was startled by a shower of silver-side minnows being pursued by blues of almost two pounds. (Tisbury Great Pond would be a splendid natural laboratory for a fisheries biologist interested in measuring the bluefish's capacity to survive and thrive in low-salinity water.)

Those who live on or near the pond are aware of the fish it often holds captive. During World War II, about two weeks after my parachute infantry division jumped into Holland in September, my company was pulled off the front lines for a few days of rest in an apple orchard, where I received a V-Mail letter from my father, who wrote that he was catching five-pound striped bass on his fly rod at the mouth of the pond's Deep Bottom Cove.

On our second visit to the pond this fall, Jesse and I discovered that the snappers weren't where they had been on our first trip, so we beached our canoe and walked along the shore, each in a different direction, casting small silver jigs every few yards. Jesse, who is a skilled and persistent angler, found the snappers before we were a half mile apart.

"Gramp, they are twice as big as the ones we caught the other day," he said as I came up to him.

They averaged three-quarters of a pound, and we soon had enough for a substantial repast for both households. We also caught six or seven striped bass, the largest about twenty inches. They were far short of the minimum length limit of twenty-eight inches, but they were challenging on our ultralight spinning rods.

Late in the day, heavy clouds gathered, the southwest wind picked up, whitecaps formed on the pond, and I was about to suggest that we head for home when I hooked a fish that felt like neither a bluefish nor a striper. As I was pondering its identity, it jumped three times, looking much like an adult shad. It was, I discovered after beaching it, a hickory shad of more than two pounds. We caught five more in the next half hour.

Once again the pond had surprised me. The shad were my first taken from its waters. They might have wandered in after spawning in a stream on nearby Cape Cod, only to have the door close behind them.

Wanting to experiment with smoking shad, I kept four of them and we raced the gathering murk across the pond as small flocks of westward-bound green-winged teal went by overhead. *(November 29, 1998)*

A YOUNG ANGLER'S INTRODUCTION

TO THE FOOD CHAIN

By Peter Kaminsky

WAINSCOTT, N.Y. — Nothing that is eaten remains alive.

Even though this truism is obvious to all, the reality that the survival of one living thing can only be ensured by the death of another is a fact of life rarely observed in our modern world. The connection between food on the plate and a living creature in the field, in the skies, or in the sea is, for most city kids, just an abstraction.

This fact was brought home to my thirteen-year-old daughter, Lily, and me during a recent walk on the beach in Wainscott, on Long Island. In the hot and humid intermezzo between the challenging and often rewarding sight-fishing of early summer and the first of the autumn feeding frenzies, the fishing is, at best, a sometime thing.

But every now and then a pack of bluefish manages to pen up a pod of baitfish, and for a few minutes here and a few minutes there, the ocean rouses from its late-summer slumber to a scene of tumult.

Lily and I, with nothing much to do, took a stroll down the beach, about a mile, to Georgica Pond. A southwest breeze tempered the withering heat and humidity, and the surge of the incoming tide sloshing around our ankles felt splendidly cool. We talked of her friends at summer camp (sorely missed) and her sister's departure for college (ditto), mixed in with the unimportant small talk that makes idle summer hours so delicious.

Just as we were about to return to the beach house of our friend Josh Feigenbaum, some movement caught my attention. About two hundred yards west of us, a swarm of terns began to mass and flutter their wings as they held position over something going on beneath them. Then one dived, and another, and another. They wheeled and re-formed for another sortie, and another, and another.

It could only be one thing: "Bluefish for sure, Lily! Let's grab a rod!"

Fumbling through Josh's tackle box, I retrieved a productive lure, the Hopkins, with a rusty, but still sharp, treble hook. I tied on a wire leader and clipped on the lure, and we sprinted down the beach. When we reached the mayhem at the water's edge, we could see baitfish leaping from the water in a spray of silver droplets and, like deathly shadows behind them, hundreds of bluefish feeding with ravenous abandon.

❖   ❖   ❖

Lily, who casts reasonably well, could not quite reach the action, so I took the rod from her, tossed a cast into the eye of the storm, and handed her the rod. As instructed, she reeled in. Within moments a bluefish struck hard.

Next came the what-do-I-do-now moment that all novice anglers experience when the pleasant enough idea of fishing becomes the reality of a living thing fighting for its life at the other end of the line.

Often, people will point the rod at the fish and reel in nonstop. This puts none of the force of the rod into the fight, and gives the fish the opportunity to pull more and more line from the reel while you strip its gears. This is a natural, and the most common, reaction.

To her credit, even in the heat of battle, Lily followed my

instructions to pull up and reel down, thus tiring the fish and recovering line.

Then came the next what-do-I-do-now moment as the fish emerged from the sea foam and flopped around on the beach. Lily opted for returning the fish, so, with some difficulty, I extracted the lure from its mouth and released it.

The birds followed the school slowly eastward. We changed the lure for a single hook.

Now the action was directly in front of a group of middle-aged women, strolling along the beach.

We cast again, and Lily fought another fish to the beach. This time, though, I wanted to keep it for dinner.

"Get me a nice piece of driftwood," I said, and Lily ran above the high-tide mark, returning with a cudgel-sized stick. I whacked the fish over the head, killing it instantly. Lily's mood changed at this point. She was disturbed by the violence and felt sympathy for the fish.

"What kind of fish are they?" one of the women asked.

"Blues," I said. "Would you like to catch one?"

"I never have, but why not?" the woman said.

I cast again, handed over the rod, and the woman, who introduced herself as Patricia, caught her first bluefish. I clunked this one, too, and Lily and I returned home.

"I like the catching part, but I don't like the killing," Lily said. My protestations that we were about to have a great meal of the freshest fish did nothing to counteract her misgivings.

At home, I filleted the fish and, to justify myself by making a point about the circle of life, or something like that, I took the carcasses down to the water and tossed them in, explaining to Lily that this would feed other fish and birds.

She was unmoved.

Then, as I washed out the sink, my wife noticed some of

the little silversides that our bluefish had gulped down for their last supper. "Look, Lily," I said as I showed her a palmful of dead baitfish, "the bluefish must have killed a thousand of these little fish. I mean, it's as much a killer as we are."

She took a small fish, examined it, and returned it to me.

I returned to the kitchen, heated some butter in a pan, seasoned the fish with salt and pepper, and cooked it in just a few minutes. Then it was a matter of spreading some mayo on toast, laying some lettuce on top followed by a slice of tomato, plump with August sweetness, and finally the cooked fish. The result was a few fine-looking bluefish, lettuce, and tomato sandwiches. After some visible internal debate, Lily picked up a half sandwich, took a bite, and pronounced our Long Island BLT a success. *(August 31, 2003)*

ANGLERS IN SEARCH OF

FALSE ALBACORE

By Stephen Sautner

A HARD-CORE SURF fisherman from Sea Bright, New Jersey, once complained about how a false albacore had grabbed a popping plug intended for a big striper, then proceeded to empty his reel in one very long, fast, and unstoppable run. "Crazy thing stripped out all my line," he said in what sounded like a tone of suppressed awe.

Not too many seasons ago, the false albacore remained mostly a mystery among surfcasters in the Northeast, its very name sounding vague and unsure. Anglers would spot the silvery schools in the fall, chasing baitfish and squirting like mercury beyond the breakers. But few would ever hook into one or even realize that they weren't some strain of incredibly fast and fussy bluefish.

But, occasionally, a rod would bend and a fisherman would stare in disbelief as his reel became a blur of vanishing line. Fifteen minutes later a crowd would have gathered on the beach around what looked like a miniature bluefin tuna of perhaps ten pounds — complete with a sickle tail and pale finlets. Then came arguments over what to call it, some insisting it was a bonito, others calling it a "little tunny."

❖   ❖   ❖

Somewhere along the way, it was discovered that false albacore would sometimes hit small bucktails or spoons if reeled at

164

breakneck speeds. About the same time, fly-rodders began hooking them on saltwater streamers. In short order, the false albacore quickly evolved into one of the premier fish among surf anglers in the mid-Atlantic and southern New England.

Now, throughout the fall, from Cape Cod to the Outer Banks, anglers patiently wait for cold fronts, which send albacore schools racing along beaches and into inlets in their pursuit of sand eels, silversides, and rainfish. Guides specialize in albacore fishing while arguments spring up over whether they fight better than the far more glamorous bonefish.

There are two schools of thought in surfcasting for false albacore. One is to literally run after the schools when they surface; the other is to wait for the fish to come to you. Having tried both, I can recommend the former only if you can sprint at thirty-five miles an hour, in waders, while false-casting.

The latter is far more enjoyable. You stand on the beach, rod in hand, searching for "sea signs," such as dimpling bait or wheeling terns. The air is crisp, and strings of migrating sanderlings weave and twist down the beach, looking surprisingly like the schools of silversides you see in the waves in front of you.

If you're incredibly blessed, a pod of albacore might erupt fifty feet away and allow a well-placed cast. But, more often than not, you'll spend a pleasant morning gazing at the waves and waiting for a fish that never shows up.

Three years ago, I watched my cast unroll and my fly touch down as if guided by magic, dead center among twenty porpoising albacore. I stripped twice and the fly stopped dead. Fly line suddenly exploded from my stripping basket, shot through the guides of my rod, and emptied into the sea, followed by half the backing on my reel.

When I finally tailed the fish — about an eight-pounder —

my hands were knotted in cramps, and sweat poured down my back. Pound for pound, it may have been the strongest fish I had ever hooked.

In fact, albacore fight so hard that they often cannot be released alive. Well-intentioned anglers sometimes spend many minutes trying to revive a fish that may swim off feebly, only to settle to the bottom a few yards away to become crab food.

Here's the secret: contrary to popular fishing lore, false albacore make fine eating, but they must be immediately bled, filleted, and iced. Like many tuna, albacore have a specialized, thick muscle used for super-fast bursts of speed, which gives off enough heat to spoil the flesh if not cooled. After icing, the fillets can be cut into cubes, dunked in a marinade of olive oil, soy sauce, white wine, and ginger, grilled, then finally eaten while resting one's own overheated muscles. *(October 25, 1997)*

IS THIS ALBACORE HEAVEN?

NO, IT'S JUST THE OUTER BANKS

By Peter Kaminsky

I F THE VAGABOND false albacore that cruise our shores on their way to winter grounds rouse your angling lust, you will be hopelessly lovesick once you encounter the albies of North Carolina's Outer Banks. Stronger than, but just as fast as, their northern relatives, they are, on average, twice as big. A fish of twenty pounds is not uncommon.

Fly-rodding for albies at Cape Lookout is in many ways the invention of one man, the retired law professor and angling author Tim Earnhardt of Raleigh, North Carolina. A lifelong freshwater fly-fisherman, he first caught the odd albie when he started fly-fishing the North Carolina coast in the 1970s. It was not until the mid-eighties that he had an angling epiphany when he realized that albacore were more catchable on small flies than on the large ones he had been using. He became an albacore addict. It took four or five years for word of the great fishing he had found to spread through the fly-fishing community, but by this season, Cape Lookout had become a place of pilgrimage for saltwater fly-fishers.

Three weeks ago, I arrived at Harker's Island Fishing Center. Fly-rod skiffs nuzzled into their slips. Guides — with beards that ranged from two-day stubble to permanent fur — loaded coolers, filled gas tanks, and traded information.

They sat relaxed on a bench outside the door of the bait shop, sipping an early-morning Coca-Cola. At their feet, an equally laid-back golden retriever chewed happily on some cast-off nautical supplies.

My cell phone rang. It was our host, Paul Dixon, asking if I was lost. Dixon, one of the first and ablest albacore fly-fishermen in Montauk, was part of a squadron of fly-rod guides who had converged on Harker's Island from points as distant as Cape Cod and Key Largo. I experienced a moment straight out of the film *Clueless* as I looked up from my phone and saw Dixon standing about ten feet from me, talking into his cell phone.

With greetings out of the way, we motored down the channel in Dixon's twenty-one-foot Seacraft. Its high prow easily breasted the building seas. No sooner had we left the inlet than my fishing partner, Josh Feigenbaum of Manhattan, spotted a school of birds.

"There's albacore under them," Dixon reported as he put down his binoculars and leaned on the throttle. We bounced over the incoming waves. Dixon cut the engines when we neared the school.

Feigenbaum took the bow, forcing me to backcast from the stern. No matter; on the second or third cast, we were both fast to fish. They ripped line like bonefish. They fought back like blues. Feigenbaum and I maneuvered back and forth on the deck, trying not to cross lines. About ten minutes later we boated two fish, of twelve and fifteen pounds.

The surface feeders went down. Paul fired up the engines, and within ten minutes we had joined a flotilla of boats about a quarter mile from the beach. We set up a chum line with glass minnows.

For two hours, we caught fish. Even though I was using a beefy 10-weight rod, the fish fought hard and my arms ached. I discovered new contortions that allowed me to reel first with one hand, then the other. When we had caught our fill, we made for the horizon, where a shrimper was lifting its nets. Diving gulls told a tale of fish feeding in the wake of the trawler.

We backed up behind the boat. Three men in orange waterproof overalls and jackets heaved unwanted fish overboard, and albies slashing in the surface added to the mayhem. We drifted behind the trawler and hooked another four fish.

❖   ❖   ❖

The wind was coming up and the seas were building. The National Weather Service called for worsening conditions, so we made for the shelter of the bight by Cape Lookout Light. The tide had changed, and with it the albacore appeared once more on the surface. For an hour and a half we chased pods of fish. So did every other boat within ten miles, there being no other protected water.

"Don't point with your rods," Dixon commanded. "Everyone else will know you have seen fish." As it turned out, the fish were so finicky and the fishing boats were so packed together, we caught only two albacore. Still, seeing them leap like blue footballs, slashing the surface like razors, was worth the time and trouble.

We called it a day. On the way back to the main highway, I recalled a saying that Bob Pasfield, the proprietor of Harker's, had shared in explanation of the great number of churches we had noticed that morning. "If this part of North Carolina is the Bible Belt," he recited, "then Harker's Island is its buckle." As we drove out, we saw a church with a black lettered signboard testifying to this truth: JESUS FIRST. OYSTERS SECOND.

Perhaps, I thought, albacore will round out an Outer Banks trinity. *(December 5, 1999)*

BABY TARPON PROVIDE
EVERGLADES CHALLENGE

By Stephen Sautner

EVERGLADES NATIONAL PARK, FLA. — Somewhere among the endless mangrove forests and sawgrass prairies of North America's last tropical wilderness lies a brackish-water creek filled with baby tarpon — fish in the five-to-thirty-pound range that have perhaps never seen a fly. I found this out last year from a fishing guide I met in the Florida Keys who had returned from a sort of busman's holiday.

He described the creek as rarely fished and "just loaded" with tarpon. When he explained how it could be reached by canoe, it grabbed top billing and finally forced my recent trip to south Florida.

Perhaps it was Van Campen Heilner's classic story "The River of Thrills," about fishing in the jungles of Cuba, that had me convinced that the proper way to catch a tarpon was not from a bridge or even poling along a flat, but from a tiny boat in a lonely, mangrove-lined creek. It sounded as pure as fishing for striped bass in a pounding November surf or casting a tiny dry fly to rising trout on a Pennsylvania spring creek.

Before I headed into the Everglades, I had spent a few nights priming myself by wrestling with monster-size tarpon on heavy spinning tackle from a roaring cut in Marathon Key, to the south. Some of those fish were true brutes of up to

100 pounds, but they seemed almost phantomlike, jumping in the shadows cast by the nearby Overseas Highway before easily breaking me off.

※　　　※　　　※

Now, with nothing but an 8-weight fly rod and a box of tarpon streamers, I silently paddled a canoe through a long canal lined by an impenetrable wall of foliage draped with Spanish moss. From what the guide had told me a year earlier, my destination lay about four miles ahead. Calls of pig frogs and the squawk of an occasional heron had replaced the din of the Overseas Highway. Heilner would have been proud, I thought.

Even in the canal a few tarpon rolled on the surface. I stopped and briefly cast for them, but remained distracted by the lure of the creek. After all, this was where real fishing guides went on their days off. I left the fish behind and continued on.

The canal emptied into a fair-sized bay about a mile wide. Rafts of wintering coots splashed and chattered noisily on the surface of the brownish water. I turned left as the guide had said, and headed along the shoreline.

A few hundred yards ahead, a white stake marked the mouth of the creek, which turned out to be part of the network of canoe trails that crisscross much of the Everglades. As I paddled closer, the entrance seemed impossibly small, just a tunnel in the mangroves, not even ten feet wide. But I glided in anyway, feeling as though the Everglades had just swallowed me without a trace, canoe and all.

※　　　※　　　※

It was otherworldly in there — dark, humid, close. Huge orb weaver spiders hung from webs strung across the aerial roots of mangroves inches from my head. A lone Louisiana heron seemed to stare down at me from its perch in disbelief. The creek itself actually appeared to be getting smaller. It twisted along at impossible angles, sending the canoe bumping from one bank to the other. Fly-casting in such a place remained impossible.

Then the first mosquito arrived, followed by another, then a few hundred more. And although I'm sure that Heilner, a pioneering angler who had fished throughout much of the tropics, would have continued on, I had quickly seen enough. I managed to turn the canoe around, and, somewhat frantically, bushwhacked my way back into the bay.

Did I take a wrong turn, or had I become the victim of a guide's joke, played on a nonpaying customer trying to glean a couple of free tips? If it was a hoax, maybe I could pass it on to another fisherman, a sort of Everglades-style snipe hunt.

By now I had already made my way back to the mouth of the canal. Another tarpon rolled in front of me, one of just a handful I had spotted during the day.

Exasperated, I halfheartedly stripped out a few yards of line, shooting a bright green streamer beneath an overhanging branch. I immediately felt a hard take and watched dumbfounded as a tarpon of about twenty pounds threw itself from the surface, rattling its gills and crashing back into the dark water.

The fish jumped again and again, shining silver and purple against the dark green of the mangroves. Each time it leapt, I lowered the rod, giving it slack so it couldn't break the line. Even though this was the first tarpon I had ever hooked on a fly rod, I had run the moment through my head so many times that it all felt well rehearsed.

Eventually the tarpon tired. It rolled on its side next to the boat, staring at me with its huge eye. I reached down to remove the hook, but the fish would have none of it. It unleashed with a final crazed leap, throwing the fly back into the canoe.

And although none of this happened on the creek I had dreamed about for the past year, suddenly I felt as if I had already been there. *(May 9, 1999)*

ODD WATERS

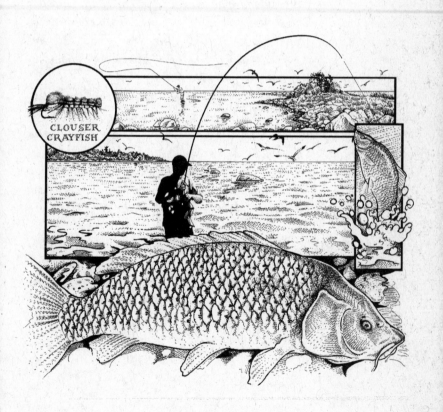

CLOUSER
CRAYFISH

Herein lurk the strange and forgotten: backwater fishing holes that won't make any fishing magazine's "Top Ten Hottest Spots"; bizarre angling methods that feel downright illicit. Then there are the fish themselves, some familiar, others covered in spines or giant scales — or no scales at all — looking as if they came from the pages of science fiction or were conjured up by Dr. Seuss.

Like cult movies, angling's B-list of "lesser" species have extremely loyal and diverse followings, such as the legions that chase sea-herring around New York City. When herring are in, certain piers in Brooklyn can feel as though the General Assembly of the UN has let out for the day for a field trip. Techniques, too, can be highly regional. Take ice-fishing, for example, eyed suspiciously by many anglers back east, but considered nothing short of high religion in the Midwestern states.

And for those who would rather stand shoulder-to-shoulder in the catch-and-release water of a crowded trout stream, unconvinced of the leaping ability of a long-nosed gar or the challenge of dry-fly fishing for redbreast sunfish (aka "pool robins"), you may need to get out more. Then again, the few who seek these out-of-the-way places might prefer you to remain just where you are.

IN DEFENSE OF FISHING

WINTER'S FROZEN PONDS

By John Waldman

ICE-FISHING IS a supremely unaffected and forth-right endeavor, one that rarely invokes the romance or introspective rambling of, say, fly-fishing. I know of only two lyrically written ice-fishing stories, and one of them is titled "Ice Fishing, the Moronic Sport."

Especially now, with the weather warming, the common view of many New York–area anglers who do not venture onto frozen lakes is that ice-fishing is a form of masochism only one step removed from self-flagellation with icicles. An act of utter desperation, the domain of stoic Minnesotans with their endless winters, but not for those in more temperate climes where spring seems just around the corner.

And yet, in late December, there are those who cannot wait for the first arctic air masses to settle over the New York City reservoir system so this underappreciated pastime can be enjoyed. This January was a tease, beginning with such pro-nounced warmth that my neighbor's forsythia bloomed. Then, in midmonth, La Niña's curvaceous jet stream jagged eastward, pulling down northern air, and the ice began to crystallize.

My first trip was to a cove on Muscoot Reservoir that provides the earliest good ice of the season. But it was a nerve-racking time spent on only two inches of ice — the bare mini-mum for safety — my anxiety fueled by a large hole that could have been made by someone falling through the day before.

Two weeks later I drove back to central Westchester County with my ice-fishing partner, Dave Taft, to explore new locations on the reservoirs. We were startled to find well over a foot of support, uncommon at the latitude, where in recent years ice was so ephemeral as to last only days at a time.

We were geared to jig for panfish, a technique that requires surprising finesse for such rugged conditions. Many ice-anglers instead put out tip-ups — awkward wooden contraptions from which baits are dangled and signal strikes with flags that spring upward. Once the tip-ups are placed, there isn't much to do but wait — for something that often never arrives — making for a dull experience.

By contrast, jigging is positively compelling. It requires a short, highly sensitive wisp of a rod, light line, and tiny metal lures in weights with large denominators: $\frac{1}{32}$, $\frac{1}{48}$, and $\frac{1}{64}$ ounce. The jigs are tipped with baits that, to warm-weather anglers, seem truly esoteric: several kinds of grubs and maggots widely available from inland tackle shops. My favorites are mousies. Named for their rodentlike tails, they are about as cute as fly larvae can possibly be.

After the hole is drilled with a handheld auger or chopped with an old-fashioned spud, the offering is lowered to the bottom and then softly quivered upward until fish are found. Although one can relax, sit, and fish through a hole for hours, Zen-like concentration is required. Hits are subtle, sometimes nothing more than a twitch of the line, and are often sensed rather than felt, akin to nymphing on a trout stream.

Unless one is unduly lucky, numerous holes must be opened and tried, a bit like wildcatting for oil, but strike it right and the fish come gushing.

Through the morning, Dave and I tried a series of bays and channels on Muscoot and Cross River Reservoirs, but with poor results. By early afternoon we felt less venturesome, and traveled to the ever-reliable cove on the Muscoot. There we enjoyed steady action with colorful, saucer-sized bluegills, but the opportunities opened by the uncharacteristically thick ice left me restless. I persuaded Dave to try a little more prospecting, this time for the big yellow perch that are caught in the main trunk of the reservoir, well outside of the cove, when the ice allows.

I looked at an underwater map of the reservoir, and by crudely sighting a line between an island and a point of land, I placed us in the general vicinity of a shallow-water reef surrounded by deep water.

❧   ❧   ❧

In the midst of this unblemished horizontal vastness, Dave was unduly lucky — he randomly drilled just one hole — but it was a gusher. In the next hour he landed one fat-bellied perch after another, losing two of the largest that snapped his line.

With February's early sunset fast approaching, we decided to complete the day back in the cove, hoping that its well-known but inconsistent evening bite of black crappie might round out our catch. We settled over our portals to the underwater world, landing a few crappie and other panfish through the next hour.

When dusk turned to darkness, we hiked off the lake in a sharpened chill that lent a crunchiness to our footsteps, piercing the midwinter silence.

We did not feel moronic at all, and in fact we were downright enlightened by having spent another day on the ice. *(February 26, 2000)*

LOOKING FOR A GOOD FIGHT?

GO LOOKING FOR A CARP

By Bob Butz

Traverse City, Mich. — A fly-fisherman prowling the northern Michigan shoreline, with its miles of secluded beaches and glistening blue water under a sky like mother-of-pearl, could easily imagine himself in the Caribbean, or perhaps wading the reefs around Christmas Island or the flats off the coast of Belize. The Lake Michigan coast is that picturesque. And, come summer, the angling is that good owing to the most unlikely of fishes: the simple and unassuming carp.

The local guide Dave McCool calls them golden bones, or the poor man's bonefish. But take it from someone who knows: though the scenery here and the quality of fishing compare favorably to those exotic locations down south, when it comes to downright power and fight, a bonefish doesn't have much on a thirty-pound carp.

McCool, a small-stream trout specialist for the better part of the year, has these waters to himself in the summer. Few boats can navigate on the boulder flats where the carp like to spawn and feed. And not many people fish for carp anyway, let alone fly-fish for them.

In fact, I know more fly-fishers who have boated permit (the most coveted saltwater species) than have landed one modest carp. Maybe because carp are considered to be not very beautiful fish that inhabit not very beautiful places.

But on a recent summer afternoon in the shallows of Lake Michigan, I would not have wanted to be any other place. The rolling waves lapping against the shore and the cries of the herring gulls soaring overhead were indicative of all things coastal. Indeed, the Great Lakes are truly like inland seas.

Here, dozens of rocky, fingerlike shoals extended off-shore. Good places to wade. Good places to sight-fish. Almost immediately, we spotted the carp — easily twenty-to-thirty-pounders — cruising alone and in pairs in less than two feet of water.

I have seen carp in rivers countless times, but never gave casting to them a second thought. Fishermen don't offer flies to carp. Disrespected as trash fish, carp are maligned by the fly-fishing elite and said to be the target of slack-jawed, bait-fishing yokels. Only in Europe is the carp prized as a fighter, the most intelligent and finicky of all freshwater gamefish.

McCool recommends black Woolly Buggers, Clouser Crayfish, and Wiggle Nymphs when the schools are feeding in the shallows. Cast in front of an oncoming fish, he suggests, and let the fly sink. The presentation is a simple affair, a series of subtle strips. McCool's advice: try to envision the fly scuttling along the bottom. Set your drag loose for after the take.

A word about the violence of the strike: imagine casting your fly into rush-hour traffic, the jolt of snagging the bumper of a runaway cab. If the fish doesn't snap your puny 8-pound leader — indeed, break your flimsy rod off at the butt-section — the initial hit can be wrenching.

And as for the ensuing fight, consider that the line capacity of the average 7-to-8-weight reel is taken up by 200 to 300 yards of backing. After most fly-fishermen wind this up, how many ever do the kind of fishing that takes them that deep into the reel again?

But every fish landed and released with McCool — twelve and not one under fifteen pounds — took me well into the Dacron line on the first run and for the duration of each fight. Upon the strike, each fish seemed to torpedo away for the shores of Wisconsin somewhere beyond the horizon, the neon-colored fly line disappearing after them as if shot from a laser beam.

We fished the leeward side of a prominent rocky outcrop where the water pooled smooth and crystal with the clarity of a lagoon. Scrutinizing every fish-shaped boulder just under the surface, we worked our way slowly toward the shoal's windy tip. And there a school of carp numbering perhaps a thousand finned and porpoised into deeper water where it required a long double-haul of the line to reach them.

When the waves rolled, we could see the giant olive zeppelin-shaped carp holding on the bottom almost vertically, mouth down and tail often out of the water. Getting them to take in this feeding position was simply a matter of getting the fly down to them.

Indeed, I spent more time reclaiming line while fighting fish than trying to get one to bite. The carp were in the mood, as they say. And I fished for them with the intensity you muster when the fishing is good — maybe even the best you've ever had. *(August 19, 2001)*

LOOKING FOR SHAD WITH THE ROAR

OF EIGHTEEN-WHEELERS NEARBY

By Stephen Sautner

It's a spot where downshifting eighteen-wheelers drown out the roar of a nearby rapids; where roadside trash — coffee cups, fast-food containers, and the tread of an occasional blown tire — litters the narrow fishermen's trail that runs along the riverbank; where getting there isn't half the fun — it's no fun at all. A friend calls it the "world's ugliest shad pool."

The only place comparable is the power-plant pool in Trenton. That spot, a rectangular dead-end canal off the lower Delaware River, attracts the first shad fishers of the season — hard-core anglers who don't let things like piles of coal and belching smokestacks distract them from casting their darts and spoons. I fished there once years ago from Jim Leedom's boat. We would cast toward shore into a steaming plume of warm water. By day's end, we brushed a fine layer of coal dust from the boat's deck and our shoulders.

We haven't fished there since, and now spend the early season upriver, casting into rushing pools chilled by snowmelt, instead of warmed by turbines. Sometimes we hear reports of fast fishing at the power plant, but have learned to shrug them off like bad habits given up long ago.

But this year the lower river failed to produce, except for a few small bucks — male shad lacking the prized roe of the females. When the run proceeded north, I followed it, but always seemed to arrive in between migrating schools. Shad fishing is all about timing; one day the river is black with fish, the next morning you could be miles off the mark.

Which is how I wound up driving to the ugly shad pool in the shadow of the interstate. I had originally decided to spend the afternoon casting into a favorite run north of the Delaware Water Gap in northern New Jersey. As shad spots go, this one is a knockout. In the height of the season, toads trill beneath towering oaks filled with singing warblers. That day, even a bald eagle soared past. But hours of casting still yielded no shad.

Then I remembered the interstate pool, and how an elderly fisherman told me last year how shad piled into it to rest after running a series of rapids downriver. He said on a good day dozens of fish could be taken. I thought about it for a moment, took one last breath of sweet spring air, then reeled up my line before piling into my truck still clad in my waders.

I remembered where the fisherman had told me to park, and how it seemed odd because it sounded as if it was on the wrong side of the interstate. But sure enough there was an obvious dirt turnoff — the universal fisherman's parking lot — just as he said. I parked and grabbed my rod, with his next set of instructions echoing through my head: "Just follow the trail to the river. You can't miss it."

What he failed to mention was that the trail led down a steep embankment that ended at a dark and dank fifteen-foot-high culvert that ran under the highway. I peered inside and could at least see light at the other end. So I wandered in, obviously blinded by the promise of fish.

It soon became apparent that I had stumbled into a local teen hangout. Graffiti covered the walls, including the requisite huge marijuana leaf, spray-painted Day-Glo green, the color of my shad dart.

By the time I emerged, the garbage-strewn trail suddenly didn't look half bad. I followed it through thick stands of poison ivy and past discarded McDonald's bags, empty Pennzoil cans, and the orange shards of an unlucky traffic cone. The roar of the highway just a few yards away, along with the faint smell of exhaust, were constant companions.

The trail led to a rocky point along the river, which marked the head of the pool. Now, with my back to the road, it looked downright enticing, the water moving at just the right pace. I fired out my first cast into the river, timed to the growl of a particularly angry-sounding tractor-trailer.

Ten minutes passed before the first shad latched on. It zipped off a few yards of line, then cleared the river in an end-over-end jump, the signature move of a bright buck. When I brought it close, several other males followed it nearly to the bank, a peculiar habit of shad during the spawning season. Why they do it is unclear, but it usually bodes well for the fishing. I quickly released the fish — about a three-pounder — and continued casting.

Then came the deliberate take of a roe-shad that had eluded me this season. It fought the way most roes do: ponderous and reserved, yet always as if she could splinter your rod and melt your reel whenever she felt like it. This one took it easy on me, eventually allowing me to slide her up the silty bank. I removed the dart from her jaw and placed her behind a boulder. She shined purple, pink, and silver, and looked as though she weighed a little over five pounds.

In the next hour, two more hard-fighting bucks came, as well as several missed strikes. The first headlights could be seen glinting through the trees up the embankment. I took the big shad from behind the boulder and headed down the trail, the ever-present roar of trucks drowning out the sound of the river, but not the unseen highway of shad that flowed beneath it. *(May 4, 2003)*

COLD MONTHS BRING A FISH A
GRANDFATHER COULD LOVE

By Dave Taft

T O THE BEST of my recollection, what my grandfather wanted most from a family gathering was
pickled herring and a seat at the table near a grand-
child or two. I never questioned his seating choices, but I
wondered about his fish. Pickled herring was the perfect ac-
companiment to any meal, with large turkeys, asparagus, even
barbecue. To my grandfather, herring was a comfort food as
basic as apple pie.

From his seat at the table, my grandfather patiently
watched me become a fisherman. He heard more than he
wanted to about fishing for snappers and about how to rig bait
for sunfish at summer camp. I bored him with the finer points
of hooks and bobbers, with stories about early-morning fishing from one shore or another. My grandfather never fished,
but through hours of talk, he laughed his thick Polish laugh
and ate herring. Mercifully for him, he died before I learned to
fly-fish.

There is nothing that reminds me of my grandfather as
much as tramping through the patchy snow of Brooklyn's Canarsie Pier to fish for herring. Fortunately for fishing addicts
like me, herring numbers peak locally during the bleak midwinter months. It is a very do-it-yourself kind of fishing. There
are no famous herring guides, no frantic late-night phone calls

from famous friends with boats, announcing herring blitzes out east. There is just harsh simplicity.

If it is winter and it is cold, it is worth a trip to see if the herring are in at Canarsie Pier. This year, my first three December trips resulted in no fish. Arriving for my last visit, I expected more of the same. But as I parked, three crows peered down suspiciously from a scraggly maple at a pile of pearlescent scales in the snow — the surest sign that herring were in. I rigged up quickly and joined a dozen other fishermen at the pier's edge.

In Canarsie, fishers from Poland, Puerto Rico, Jamaica, Korea, Russia, and countries whose accents I don't recognize fish for herring almost all winter. It warms me each year to hear my grandfather's laugh echoed by more-recent immigrants. This time, a man named Larry kidded me in a heavy Russian accent that I had already missed most of the action. A Korean gentleman smiled repeatedly, but knew no more English than "fish, fish," as he craned herring after herring over the pier's railings.

Fishing for herring requires more fortitude than skill. The light lines and rods and the tiny hooks make it seem more like freshwater fishing. Heavier tackle is usually used in saltwater. The fish feed on tiny shrimp and plankton, so lures tied to catch them are flashy things measuring less than an inch and tied with silvered hooks, bits of tinsel, and bright fabric. A string of them may measure almost five feet. The fanciest of these rigs includes hooks molded in plastic to look like tiny shrimp, or even tiny glow-in-the-dark phials that serve to attract the herring from their deep-water homes. Sadly for the makers of tackle, little is necessary to catch a herring, and less is usually more.

The process is fairly simple. First, buy a herring rig from the local tackle shop. Actually, buy two or three, because there are plenty of snags at the bottom of Jamaica Bay. Buy a few small sinkers and ask about the tides. This is more polite than important. Herring bite according to their own unknowable schedule, sometimes when the tide is coming in, sometimes when it is going out. The oldest fishing adage plainly applies, though: You can't catch a fish if your line isn't in the water.

So, head directly to the pier, tie a weight to the bottom of your rig, tie your rig to the end of your fishing line, and lower it all to the bottom. Wait. Wait some more. Jiggle the rod a little. Wait some more. Talk to your neighbor. Pour coffee from a thermos. Drink the coffee. Joke with your neighbor. Wait a little longer.

It is hard to imagine what form of deep-sea creature a herring fly could possibly imitate, or, for that matter, what a five-foot rig of them swimming jerkily across the icy, black current could represent, but herring love herring rigs. At some point in the wait, you will feel a pronounced tug. When you do, reel in your line and admire the beautiful Atlantic herring, *Clupea harengus*.

Each herring is a marvel of adaptation, streamlined and silvery purple. One look into its huge dark eyes and you may wish to throw it back to swim again. That is always your choice.

Should you choose to keep what you catch, there are dozens of herring recipes. People who do not like fish have told me that the best way to prepare pickled herring is to fillet them, then place them in kosher salt with a brick on top to weigh them down. After three days of curing, throw away the fillets and eat the brick.

There are people like my grandfather, though, who preferred the fillets, particularly when removed from the salt and marinated in wine vinegar, onions, and mustard seed. For me, herring chunks served on crackers in a vinegar cream sauce with onions take me a long way back to family dinners with my grandfather. *(January 12, 2003)*

SPINEFISH APLENTY IN
WATERS OF THE EAST

By Ray Ottulich

I REMEMBER THE time several years ago when I sat in a car as we wound up the twisting two lanes of a small gorge between the Hudson and the flanks of the Catskill Mountains. Gazing down and taking inventory, in fly-fishing guide fashion, of the frantic frothing waters rushing between deep, dark pools, I asked nonchalantly how the fishing was.

The answer was quick and unexpected: "There's no fish in there."

Since I was just on a short visit, and this was the East, I swallowed all my usual questions and chalked the reason up to some type of invisible pollution.

Now, as I continue my fly-rod explorations of these wild lands and waterways that flow from trout water to tidewater, I've discovered rivers, creeks, and kills teeming with wild fish. Some are natives, others invaders, and yet I've respectively come to group them under the sobriquet of "spinefish," in honor of their warm-water habitats, their aggressive behavior, and the intimidating dorsal fins of sharp, skin-piercing spines that jut fiercely above their backs.

The king of these spinefish and one of the most renowned fly-rod catches in this part of the world is the anadromous *Morone*

saxatilis, or striped bass. Returning after twenty-four years spent in Montana, I've really noticed the change in New York, especially the clearer air and cleaner water. Federal laws and the efforts of the Hudson Estuary Fisheries Recovery Program and other dedicated organizations are making the difference.

Striped bass once again ascend the Hudson estuary from the Atlantic in the spring, voraciously pursuing blueback herring, alewife, and shad until they, too, succumb to reproductive urges at the convergence of optimal temperature and the length of daylight. A cool spring keeps them in the estuary longest, and within casting distance of fly-rodders along some of the spawning tributaries entering the Hudson.

Stripers will shadow bluebacks (which like fast currents and rocky bottoms) in these creeks and kills at least up to the first barrier (they won't leap like salmon), and have been caught as far as eight miles from the estuary. Stripers commonly weigh thirty-plus pounds, a strong and formidable fish on a fly rod that had better be at least an 8-weight with a good reel.

Then there's *Micropterus dolomieu* — the smallmouth or black bass — which is found in all the same lies as trout and will aggressively attack streamer and dry flies. Premium habitats are fast, big-boulder, pocket-water runs and deep pools over broken ledge rock.

Smallmouths, interestingly, have been taking over habitat and replacing largemouth bass in the Hudson River as water quality and clarity have improved. With light rods of 3- or 4-weight, the consistent hookups and the real possibility of a two-to-four-pound fish makes smallmouthing for me as good as some of the fly-fishing I've had in Montana.

The blocky-shaped, red-eyed, brassy-brown *Ambloplites rupestris,* or rock bass, a native to the Hudson drainage, are found side-by-side with smallmouth in fast-current, rocky-bottom streams where there is plenty of shelter. When hooked, these fish put up a scrappy fight, but play out very quickly.

The slow-current, deep-water belly section of pools, with their bottoms of sand or silt-covered rubble, are home to *Lepomis auritus*, the redbreast sunfish, or "pool robin." Though of small to moderate size, they are aggressive feeders, shooting up like bullets from the depths to take dry flies in splashy rises off the surface. They are somewhat somber-shaded above, but their breast colors — yellowish in females and reddish in males — become positively vibrant during the breeding season. Use light rods, fine leaders, and nymphs, small streamers, or dry flies for these feisty five-to-eight-inch panfish.

I still hear people say from time to time, "There's no fish in there." Now I realize that what they mean is, "There's no trout in there." And if these anglers continue to choose to fish stocked trout over wild fish, their experiences will be a bit diminished, and my favorite haunts will stay a bit wilder for a little longer. *(April 29, 1999)*

FROM THE CRETACEOUS TO

A PAN NEAR YOU

By C. J. Chivers

THE CAYUGA LAKE air had been so still at night that, sitting on the porch swing, by the water, it seemed as if you might hear a car door slam two miles away. Morning broke, hot and hushed.

I stepped off the dock into cool water and muck. After a few minutes of wading, I came upon the fish near the reeds, right where they had been the day before. They looked as long as yardsticks. Now and then one rose, dimpled the surface, and eased back under, all with the slightest movement of fin.

To satisfy your expectations, I should now be telling you that these fish were trout, bass, salmon, or pike. They were none of the above.

They were long-nosed gar, waiting in ambush in the thin water and heat.

I reached into the bucket, hooked a shiner through the lips, and flipped it to the nearest fish, which snapped at it and swam off with the tiny tail hanging from its jaw. I swept the rod backward. The gar leapt from the water in a high, slashing twist, and then it bolted, a living fossil leaving behind a hearty swoosh.

It was something to tell Chipper, who would want to know.

❖   ❖   ❖

Gar are prehistoric fish — narrow-snouted, thickly armored, air-breathing, and vaguely reptilian in appearance — that have remained similar in form for 100 million years. Dr. Melanie Stiassny, curator of fishes at the American Museum of Natural History, calls the seven extant species "the last few tips of an evolutionary tree that reaches to the Cretaceous," which makes them rough contemporaries with the stegosaurus.

One species — the long-nosed — endures in New York State, residing in the St. Lawrence and Niagara Rivers, as well as Lake Ontario, Lake Champlain, and the Finger Lakes, according to Edward Woltmann, a state biologist. They may be more widespread than that, but it is hard to know. Most people pay them no mind.

This is a mistake, as Chipper McElwee and I learned.

Since childhood, McElwee and I have fished Cayuga Lake, a thirty-eight-mile-long glacial trench in central New York that we regard as our personal reserve of freshwater gamefish and food for the pan. Together we cast lures and flies and sometimes we troll slowly in a white-and-blue boat that is almost forty years old.

Chipper is the third generation of McElwees to memorize this water, and through a lifetime of trial and error he has assembled bits of fishing knowledge into patterns of plenty. He knows, with something between confidence and certainty, which shelves the trout roam in March and April, which coves hold perch in May, and which weeds and piles of rock attract bass from June through September.

Some of these bass are the stuff of daydreams, exceeding four, five, or six pounds. There were summers we fished for them until our faces ached from the squinting.

We never bothered with gar.

We had seen them over the years, of course, including some we estimated at longer than four feet. But they seemed creepy and dim, and we did little more than trade stray facts about them from old books: they are primeval; their eggs are poisonous; and one species, the alligator gar, grows longer than eight feet in the South, where men have been known to shoot them with guns.

Then came vacation and a heat wave, and I left Manhattan for a week of bass-casting and card-playing at the McElwee cottage. On a Sunday slog through the cove to catch sunfish for dinner, we noticed the gar.

What if, I more or less said.

Why not, McElwee more or less answered.

I threw jigs at them. None took.

That night, McElwee went home for work. I sat on the swing, sipping beer, listening to silence, thinking about gar. Gar have big teeth for a reason — to hold and kill fish. I decided to set aside purism and get straight to business. I would cast them live fish.

They proved willing the next day when shiners, each holding a small hook, rained down from above.

The first few fought unremarkably, even on four-pound test. But then some of the hooked gar jumped: twisting skyward, flopping sideways, sending up frothy splashes when they fell back to the lake. One jumped twice. Like a bass. Only higher.

McElwee ducked out of work and returned to the water on Wednesday, bringing with him his elephantine memory for all things related to Cayuga Lake fish.

Gar jump? He was enthused. He quickly recalled years' worth of gar sightings, and soon we puttered the boat into another cove, dropped anchor, and waded to a bar of gravel and sand. A few dozen gar milled before us, right where he said they would be.

In an hour we caught and released four or five, and

McElwee hooked a bigger one, which dashed three times for deep water before tiring at his feet. As he lifted the fish — maybe forty inches long and weighing seven or eight pounds — it thrashed and its teeth nearly raked his face.

McElwee jumped backward and dropped it. The fish broke the line.

We had spent decades coaxing secrets from this lake. We knew on that day that there would be loons on the surface between the Spring Hole and Aurora, and trout underneath them. We knew that fine bass were finning near certain rocks.

Who cared?

Long-nosed gar were in, and they were hungry.

"Give me another minnow," McElwee said, suddenly impatient. Those big bass, fodder for daydreams? They could wait. *(July 4, 2001)*

DO NOT BE ALARMED;

IT'S ONLY A PADDLEFISH

GREG THOMAS

LOOKING MORE LIKE a wicked prehistoric creature than a target of sportfishers, paddlefish provide Montana anglers with an exciting annual diversion from the norm.

And paddlefish are anything but normal, especially in the Western bastion of fly rods and dainty trout. Rather than a respectable sportfish, a paddlefish looks as though it could have climbed out of the Japanese cinema to lay waste to Tokyo.

Crowding into traditional spawning areas on far-eastern Montana's Yellowstone and Missouri Rivers (two of only three river systems in the world where the fish is found, the Yangtze drainage being the other), the paddlefish — which looks like a cross between Daffy Duck and a toothless shark — may be the closest an angler will ever come to catching a live fossil, and is older than even the gar.

A Montana resident for over 60 million years, the paddlefish was not discovered here until 1962 when a Yellowstone River angler hooked something different from a trout: "Something weird," he said.

Within a week, sixty more were landed, and by 1965 the paddlefish, with its two-foot-long spatulate bill and toothless mouth, was placed on the state's prestigious gamefish list.

❖   ❖   ❖

Today the state record stands as a 142-pounder taken from the Missouri River in 1973. That is considerably larger than Montana's state-record lake trout, which weighed only forty-two pounds.

The average paddlefish weighs between twenty-five and seventy-five pounds, with larger specimens, the egg-laden females, generally being caught later in the season than the males. While impressive in size, they pale in comparison with China's twenty-foot monsters.

Any paddlefish is large by Montana standards, where pan-sized trout reign supreme. It sets itself further apart from a trout by holding the title "vegetarian." Paddlefish do not rise to dainty flies, and they will not go for a ball of worms, either. Instead, the paddlefish, one of fewer than thirty coelacanths — a rare order of bony fishes — ever captured in the world, locates food with its bill and filters microscopic plankton from the water.

As there has yet to be an effective plankton imitation on the market, fishermen revert to crude yet effective tactics while fishing for the so-called spoonbills.

Occasionally, other fish might be found in a paddlefish's stomach, but they are most likely swallowed by accident. So the only way to hook a paddlefish is to snag it wherever possible. Montana anglers use huge saltwater rods, with the flexibility of baseball bats, to loft huge treble hooks off of 50-to-80-pound-test line. Old spark plugs are commonly used for weight.

After the treble hook hits the bottom, snaggers retrieve the line in a series of jerks, hoping that a hook may impale itself in a paddlefish; not much different from dredging for drowned bodies with grappling hooks. But in heavy current, a large paddlefish hooked in the tail is nearly impossible to catch. Depending on the size of the fish, the water temperature, and the river's stage of runoff, landing a paddlefish may take sixty seconds, or require a twenty-minute tug-of-war that the angler will never forget.

Paddlefish grow rapidly when they are young, reaching twenty-seven inches in length by their third year. By their seventh birthday, those fish may reach forty-eight inches long, and by their ninth year they measure between fifty and sixty inches and weigh forty or fifty pounds. Paddlefish, by avoiding treble hooks, northern pike, blue herons, and largemouth bass, can live thirty years or more, but their growth is extremely slow after they reach ten years old. Because of that slow growth rate, paddlefish are susceptible to overfishing. In fact, they are not abundant in much of their range because of habitat loss and exploitation; they were fished commercially for their flesh and eggs, which are turned into caviar.

Paddlefish require a free-flowing river, often with high sediment loads for successful spawning and juvenile survival. Because most free-flowing rivers have been thwarted by dams and reservoirs, most of the prime paddlefish habitat is history. But Montana's paddlefish thrive because of good spawning habitat that still exists in the lower Yellowstone and the Missouri below Fort Peck Reservoir. Montana's stocks are among the last wild stocks capable of supporting a controlled sport fishery.

Anglers who land paddlefish (each angler is allowed one fish a year on the Yellowstone, and two a year on the Missouri) should enjoy some prime eating. About 25 percent of a paddlefish is edible, and the meat is likened to scallops; it is boneless, white, and delicate after an underlayer of red flesh is removed.

However prepared, one or two paddlefish take care of special occasions for a year. And they are pursued during the big barbecue months of May, June, and July.

The paddlefish is touted as a spectacular, savage fighter, but landing one can feel more like hauling in a soggy log than fighting a prime gamefish. For acrobatics, the paddlefish is no rainbow trout. In fact, a paddlefish is more prone to hug the bottom while it's being hauled in. Rating the fight of a paddlefish versus an old boot results in a tie.

But any fish in Big Sky Country that weighs from 25 to 145 pounds is worth some backbreaking work. The result is often a close-up look at the nearest thing to a living dinosaur most anglers are likely to see. *(May 15, 1996)*

THE LOFTY MYSTERY OF
WHY STURGEON LEAP

By John Waldman

T HE STURGEON SHOT spinning out of the water like a spear, its gray flanks and white belly flashing, before crashing back and vanishing. Moments before, some enigmatic urge had compelled the great fish to aim its snout up and accelerate skyward, allowing me a sight that had long eluded me.

Over considerable time spent on the Hudson River, I had heard the loud splashes made by leaping sturgeon, but I was always looking the wrong way and had seen only the water circles that marked their reentries. This behavior is common where sturgeon are found, but it is not a sight one can plan for.

For years, the Hudson River Fisherman's Association offered a cash reward for a photo of a leaping sturgeon; no one could ever claim it. It was not until this day in Wisconsin, while walleye fishing and staring off — the right way — at Lake Winnebago's western shore, that I was treated to this visual epiphany.

Why sturgeon leap is one of the great mysteries of the fish world. Many big fish jump, but these are usually speedy, surface-oriented kinds like billfish, tuna, and tarpon. But the sturgeon is a committed bottom-dweller, a whiskered relic of a group that dominated the seas during dinosaur times but is now reduced to two dozen species worldwide, with many in peril.

The incongruity of sturgeon vaulting was noted by one observer in 1731, who wrote that "in May, June and July, the rivers abound with them, at which time it is surprising, though very common to see such large fish elated in the air, by their leaping some yards out of the water; this they do in an erect posture, and fall on their sides, which repeated percussions are loudly heard some miles distance."

Fittingly, sturgeon had brought me to Lake Winnebago and Oshkosh, Wisconsin, to attend the fourth International Sturgeon Symposium. Sturgeon, the source of the finest caviar, have become a focus of attention, so much so that the symposium drew more than four hundred scientists, with potential registrants turned away.

The news from overseas was not good: a species of sturgeon that once roamed from Scandinavian waters to the Black Sea has been reduced to one tiny population in the Gironde River in France. Other species, because of the lofty prices on their heads and rampant poaching, are being overfished in the environmentally imploding Caspian Sea.

Fortunately, the state of sturgeon is far better in North America, and perhaps nowhere more so than in Lake Winnebago. This huge and productive lake is blessed with a robust lake sturgeon population and a deeply devoted army of fishermen that years ago banded together to form a progressive conservation group, Sturgeons for Tomorrow. Although its members are among the most ardent practitioners of the arcane sport of spearing sturgeon through holes in the ice from darkened shanties, they are also tireless volunteers committed to protecting the fish.

A field trip one afternoon for symposium participants included viewing a man-made sturgeon spawning area — rock riprap at a bend in Lake Winnebago's tributary, the Wolf River.

In May the sturgeon are drawn to the shallow rubble where hundreds of sightseers admire them at an official sturgeon viewing area. Bratwurst stands are set up and a festival atmosphere pervades. To dissuade poachers, volunteers stand guard in twelve-hour shifts.

Next stop was a bridge over the river. The police had blocked off the road, allowing the biologists to crowd the crossing. Within five minutes, three Wisconsin Department of Natural Resources boats idled downriver in perfect side-by-side formation. As the twenty-to-fifty-pound sturgeon reached the bridge pool right below us, electroshocks from the boats temporarily stunned them, and the fish were netted before being carefully tagged and released.

But I remained obsessed with the sight of the airborne sturgeon. Because they are fish of considerable value, hunted for centuries, folk theories abound about why they leap. The guide on my walleye trip had heard that sturgeon eat crayfish whose claws nip the fish's intestines; the sturgeon leap to relieve the crustacean's grip. An angler said they leave the water to lose leeches and other parasites, but it takes more than a splash to shed these gruesome annoyances.

Other theories have them leaping to escape predators, or as a startle-and-fright response — both unlikely for a fish that is usually the biggest in the neighborhood. One theory has them capturing airborne prey — but they're coming off the bottom in murky water; how could they sight insects? Another theory explains the behavior as courtship or as an aid in shedding eggs during spawning — but where's the partner?

Another explanation gets closer to the soul of the fish: it simply feels good.

A new scientific theory emerged at the symposium. A group of Florida researchers believe that sturgeon leap to communicate with one another. They noted in the Suwannee River that jumping occurs primarily in summer, when sturgeon are holding in a few cool-water refuges. Most leaping happens near dawn, with a second peak at dusk, and only sporadically the rest of the day.

They found that the jump reports have a characteristic acoustic signal — "repeated percussion" — that can be heard through the air more than a half-mile away, and probably farther underwater. They surmised that sturgeon leap to help provide group cohesion among scattered individuals living in a dark and turbid environment.

So why did the sturgeon I saw leap? I'm not completely sure why. But I know that someone noticed, and was deeply moved. *(October 21, 2001)*

WHEN FISH CAME TO

THE FISHERMAN

By Stephen Sautner

M Y UNCLE PETE was the first to tell me about the vast schools of whiting that used to wash ashore each winter. "Frostfish," he called them, explaining how frenzied schools chased baitfish right into the surf, and receding waves left them flopping on the beach by the thousands.

Beachcombers from the Rockaways to Long Island's South Fork would wander along the shores at night, waiting for the next breaker to deposit a new load of glistening fish, which they would then smoke, pickle, or freeze. They built huge bonfires, hoping the light would attract baitfish, which in turn brought in the whiting. On slow nights, whole families would gather around the fires and wait out the schools.

This was secondhand information, as my uncle Pete wasn't really a fisherman and had never frostfished a day in his life. But the idea of picking fish off the beach like ripe apples excited the heck out of my older brother, Gene, and me, both in high school at the time.

I readied a stout rod and reel and a four-hook whiting rig, but took an old crab net out of the basement just in case I decided to scoop them up ten at a time.

My dad liked the idea, too. Dad was another nonfisherman, but he loved cold weather, the more frigid the better, and he frequently encouraged us to do things like go sledding when it was ten below, or take walks in ice storms. I remember how he perked up when Pete said that the coldest nights were best.

But, as it turned out, we didn't make it frostfishing that season. I don't remember why. The next year Gene got his driver's license, and decided to take me whiting fishing at a pier in New Jersey for my birthday.

While this wasn't frostfishing with spears and surf and bonfires, it still sounded like fun to catch lots of fish in chilly December. Before we left, I phoned the pier to check on the conditions. The bait-shop owner was enthusiastic, bordering on ecstatic. He talked about offshore winds, plenty of baitfish in the surf, and loads of fishermen the night before, hauling away garbage pails full of whiting.

Promising fillets for all and bundled against the cold, we headed to the frostfish grounds to cash in on the sea's bounty.

The pier was a onetime steamship dock, jutting out hundreds of feet into the Atlantic. The first half had been converted into an amusement park, complete with roller coasters, a carousel, even a haunted mansion, all closed for the winter.

Then came the bait, tackle, and coffee shop. Huge stuffed striped bass, bluefish, and weakfish hung from its walls, along with faded snapshots showing proud fishermen kneeling behind piles of whiting or snapper blues or tautog.

For bait, we bought a couple of frozen mackerel that looked and felt like wooden clubs, along with a few extra sinkers and rigs, and continued outside to the fishing area. The end of the pier was equipped with enormous floodlights that shined on the rolling ocean below. Hundreds of fishermen lined the rails, packed shoulder to shoulder and sometimes two deep. Fishing rods poked out in every direction, and lines draped into the sea like the tendrils of some huge jellyfish.

Then it occurred to us: no fish were being caught. We walked along the pier, peeking into empty buckets and garbage pails, and listened to fishermen mutter. Finally we learned what had happened.

About half an hour earlier, a fisherman told us, a whale — probably a humpback — surfaced right off the pier and proceeded to eat the evening's whiting supply. One fisherman broke his rod when his line briefly tangled on a fin. Others actually cast sinkers at the great beast, hoping to drive it away.

Upon hearing the news, Gene headed straight for the tackle shop, content to wait out the rest of the evening drinking coffee. I, on the other hand, wanted my first frostfish badly. I found a spot and cast out, and spent the next few hours in the cold watching the crowds thin and waiting for at least the whale to show up again, which it never did.

Over the next few years, the whiting schools began declining rapidly. Most people blamed it on increased commercial fishing, which cleaned out spawning stocks to the north, while others said it was some sort of natural cycle. One by one, fishing boats began sailing for other species, and tackle shops replaced whiting rigs with striped-bass plugs and bluefish lures. Even the pier mysteriously burned down one summer.

Somewhere along the way, before the stocks really crashed, I managed to sail aboard a party boat and catch my garbage pail full of whiting. I remember giving away most of my catch to the mates, realizing I had no need for 115 dead fish.

And though the topic still occasionally comes up, as far as I can tell there hasn't been any frostfishing for decades. As for me, the only December surf-fishing I do anymore is for late-season striped bass. I stand knee-deep in the breakers and cast heavy lures to swirling fish after dark. Sometimes, when the wind is offshore and the air is cold and heavy, I imagine that the next wave will bring thousands of silvery frostfish shimmering all around me. *(January 2, 1997)*

GROWING UP IN BROOKLYN, FEELING AT HOME IN ALASKA

BY DAVE TAFT

ROWING UP IN Brooklyn, my brother and I graduated from hand lines to fishing rods along the piers, bulkheads, and walkways of Sheepshead Bay. We would cast for porgies, Lafayette, snapper, flounder, and herring for hours. But we really loved the oddball fish that Peterson's *Field Guide to Atlantic Coast Fishes* would later decipher. In this manner, stargazers, windowpanes, and lizardfish all found their way into our eager young palms. At eleven years old, I could never have guessed the true trajectory of all those casts. But three decades later, I still return to these piers to bottom-fish and clear my mind.

Cordova, Alaska, is the kind of town where salmon are king and bottom fish like greenling, cod, and sculpin get no respect. My friends and I had traveled to this remote Alaskan village last fall to wade glacially fed streams, fish alongside bears and eagles, gawk at glaciers, and play in the snow.

But weeks of reading, buying, packing, and fly-tying had left my mind as cluttered as my baggage. I needed to clear my thoughts before I was ready to fish for salmon. As a commercial fishing port, Cordova has many piers, and some time on one of them seemed like the perfect way to begin this fishing adventure.

I had little idea what I might catch, but as I left for the airport, I stuffed Peterson's *Field Guide to Pacific Coast Fishes* under the layers of thermal underwear in my baggage, and tucked my trusty spinning rod in among the fancy fly-rod tubes.

In the land of big-game, fly-out fishing adventures, pier-fishing takes a back seat. On my first night in town, regulars at the Alaskan Hotel, Bar, and Liquor Store excitedly assured me that salmon were often caught from the town's piers. But when I asked about what else I might catch, the friendly faces seemed bewildered. Why would anyone bother, when salmon were jumping at the river mouths?

The next morning, Brian Marston, a fisheries biologist with the Alaska Department of Fish and Game, was far more positive. Pointing to a dock a few hundred yards from his office, he reeled off a list of fish I'd never heard of, and certainly had never fished for, beneath the docks of New York City.

It is hard to explain the mysterious appeal of bottom-fishing from piers. Fish caught this way are usually not flashy, large, or even edible, but there is always great variety. And the mystery of not knowing what has latched on to your hook is magnetic. I thought of little else but Marston's list as I positioned myself on the wooden pier. A mighty Alaskan tide was pushing water past as I tied on my favorite fish-finding rig and baited the hook with a slice of herring.

In a misty rain, gulls lounged everywhere, attracted to Old Faithful, a bubbling underwater geyser of fish offal that swirled up every ten minutes or so from the local cannery. I reasoned this Alaskan-scale bird feeder might also interest the fish.

The herring produced nothing for about half an hour. And though I was standing on a pier identical to any at Sheepshead Bay, the scenery was strictly Alaskan. I was soon under the spell of snowcapped mountains, watery-eyed harbor seals, and lolling sea otters. A pack of Steller's sea lions methodically picked off silver salmon at the harbor's entrance, savagely flinging them into the air before swallowing them whole. Eagles and ravens called.

My attention was refocused by a marbled murrelet, a chickenlike waterbird, which emerged from the water below me with a silvery, wriggling fish. Inspired, I tied on a herring rig and began to cast the tiny, shrimplike imitations into the tide. It wasn't long before I was examining my first Alaskan catch against the field guide. A single whisker under its chin, a purple hue, and separated dorsal fins identified it as a Pacific cod.

Excited now, I employed my brother's favorite pier-fishing technique, aiming my string of lures parallel to the pilings and twitching them back slowly. In a few casts, a toothy, snake-headed fish grabbed the lure. According to the field guide, it was a juvenile lingcod. This was followed by three or four more lingcod, and several white-spotted greenlings about fourteen inches long.

What grabbed the lure next defied identification. After a head-shaking tussle, I hoisted a dark brown fish of about eleven inches onto the pier. It was composed primarily of a spiny, frowning head. What body it had was covered with brown spots and splotches; its tail was something of an afterthought. Fins, both spiny and soft, radiated in every direction. It was like most bottom fish, only worse.

The sputtering rain intensified as the moving tide stilled. With only a little guilt, I kept the mystery fish, and marched back up the hill to the Department of Fish and Game, where a smiling Marston pulled a twenty-pound book off his shelf and pronounced the fish a brown Irish lord. We laughed as I left; so much for the Irish nobility. The rain had intensified by the time I reached the warmth of the Alaskan Hotel, Bar, and

Liquor Store. And slapping the wet field guide on the bar, I was adjusting to my first dry moment of the day, when one of last night's regulars cheerily asked how I had done. I told him I had caught a few, and we quietly toasted the brown Irish lord, good times, and the salmon I was only now ready to catch. *(January 6, 2004)*

SALTED VERSION OF
FLY-FISHING IS A HIT

By Robert H. Boyle

ERE WAS ERIC LEISER of Wappingers Falls, New York, a devotee of trout, a guru of fly-fishing, and the author of *Fly Tying Materials*, *The Book of Fly Patterns*, and *The Complete Book of Fly Tying* (now in its twenty-first printing, 90,000 copies sold), sitting in a fourteen-foot rowboat with a six-horsepower engine, joyously pumping a spinning rod — a spinning rod! — up and down to jig a strip of cut squid twenty feet down on the bottom of the Housatonic River where it empties into Long Island Sound.

And here was Leiser's pal Pete Zito, the proprietor of Black Canyon Flies and Supplies in Wappingers Falls and a licensed New York State guide, who takes Masters of the Universe fly-fishing on the Beaverkill, wielding, heaven help us, a spinning rod with a baited dead killie weighed down by a three-ounce sinker. "This is not catch-and-release!" Pete exclaimed. "This is the gut-'em-and-eat-'em society!" What was the world of fly-fishing purists coming to?

"A good time," said Eric, and that's true.

He and Zito were fishing for fluke, a delicious flatfish that also goes by the names of summer flounder, sole, and, if big enough, doormat. I'd gone on the trip after the end of a July heat wave to observe Leiser's extraordinarily successful fluke-fishing methods. Friends who had gone with him reported there were days when they came back with thirty to forty fluke as other boats landed only one or two.

Before launching, Leiser stopped at the Stratford Bait and Tackle Shop to get the latest intelligence from the owner, John Posh. "A lot of fluke," Posh said. But then he added that just about every fish was frustratingly short of the new fifteen-inch length limit in Connecticut.

Despite this, out we went, and we had action from start to finish. In three hours of fishing we caught more than three dozen fluke, with Leiser catching the most. But Posh was right; all but two were just short of the fifteen-inch limit. "These fluke came in from deep water as the water warmed up," Leiser said. "They're looking for food, and they find it in estuaries or along the shore, not in deep water. We'll come back when they've grown, before the season closes on September fifteenth."

Leiser's success is attributable to the very refined techniques and touches he brings to saltwater spinning from freshwater fly-fishing and fly-tying for trout. Even as a ten-year-old in Brooklyn, nearly sixty years ago, he was a fastidious angler who heated sewing needles over a gas stove so he could bend them to shape to catch goldfish in the park. "I got some up to a pound!" he exulted.

In contrast to fluke fishermen who fish heavy, Leiser goes as light as possible. For starters, take his five-foot-long, home-concocted spinning rod, which looks as if it were designed by Rube Goldberg. It consists of the broken lower half of a graphite bait-casting rod taped to the forward half of a broken Vince Cummings fly rod, with a flexible tip that sticks out seven inches.

There is a reason for such madness. "I wanted stiffness to drive the hook home," Leiser explained, hefting the rod and waving the tip like an orchestra leader, "yet I wanted a tip with some give so that when I was playing a fish, it wouldn't tear the hook out. It's also sensitive to the slightest touch, unlike a heavy boat rod. A lot of guys in fluke-fishing figure to over-power the fish, but if a fish makes a sudden lurch, the hook can tear out of the mouth."

❊   ❊   ❊

Leiser kept control of the boat so that his baited jig held bot-tom no matter which way the wind or tide changed. "The trick in fishing a depth of twenty feet or more is to feel bottom as you go along," he said. "And the way to do that is to fish with a fine line. Diameter is the most important thing, and with new lines like Spiderwire, you can get, say, twelve- or fifteen-pound-test line that has the diameter of what used to be six- or eight-pound-test line. And I use a jig as light as the current will permit, a half ounce, sometimes a quarter of an ounce. Some fishermen feel that unless they have twenty- or thirty-pound-test line, they're going to lose fish. Well, to get that line down you're going to have to use a much heavier sinker or jig, be-cause the current's going to sweep the line away because of its diameter. You're also not going to have the sensitivity needed.

"Because I was into fly-tying, I decided to imitate the fish that the fluke were feeding on. What I did was to tie white marabou, not bucktail, on the jig because marabou has a lot more life and an action similar to natural squid. I enhance that with strands of silver Mylar to add a bit of flash as an attrac-tor, and then I add a piece of squid and even a spearing on top of that. Sometimes I use a killie."

For all his expertise and the gadzillions of fluke he has caught, Leiser has yet to catch a bigger fluke than his wife June's nine-and-a-quarter-pounder or his daughter Kathleen's seven-and-a-half-pounder. "Beaten twice," he conceded, and then quickly added, "but the smaller fish are better eating." *(September 5, 1999)*

A FEAST OF WHITEBAIT
BEGINS WITH A CAST NET

By Nelson Bryant

ONE OF THE REWARDS of growing old is rediscovering pleasurable endeavors long neglected. My latest such experience involved capturing and devouring whitebait.

The unusual warmth of this past summer and fall and extensive blooms of krill altered the feeding habits and movements of striped bass along the shores of Martha's Vineyard, where I live. It became increasingly difficult for me to catch stripers from the beach with a fly rod, my favorite approach to the species. Gorging on krill — small, shrimplike crustaceans — the bass tended to ignore all flies and lures offered them. Part of my problem was an unwillingness to investigate new locations, or to visit my favorite spots at odd hours. I began fly-fishing for striped bass from the island's beaches nearly sixty years ago, and expect them to be waiting for me when I follow my traditional patterns.

In late September the man-made opening through the barrier beach that links the Vineyard's Tisbury Great Pond to the ocean was closed by a combination of wind, waves, and tidal currents — this occurs two or three times a year — and I went to the pond to see if, as often happens, substantial numbers of stripers had been trapped inside.

A few years ago I had an astonishing afternoon with the pond's captive stripers while fishing from my canoe, catching

216

and releasing bass on almost every cast for more than two hours before I reminded myself that I had all the fish I wanted for supper and the freezer, and that I was simply toying with a splendid quarry.

On this year's September visit to the pond, I saw no gulls or terns or breaking stripers, but I did see schools of Atlantic silverside minnows along the shore, in the exact spot where nearly seventy-five years ago my father had showed me how to seine them for a whitebait repast. Atlantic silversides, which grow to about three and a half inches in length, are common along the East Coast from the south side of the Gulf of St. Lawrence to Cape May, New Jersey.

Another part of a whitebait meal often netted with silversides is the slender, silvery sand eel, or sand lance.

Leaving my canoe on the beach, I went home and got my minnow seine and persuaded my companion, Ruth Kirchmeier, to join me in a whitebait quest. It takes two people to use a minnow seine, but if you know how to throw a cast net, you can go after whitebait on your own.

To quote A. J. McClane in his *Encyclopedia of Fish Cookery,* whitebait is "considered an Epicurean delight both because of its scarcity and its unusual texture."

Along both the East and West Coasts of North America, the usual candidates for a whitebait repast are silversides (sometimes called spearing) and sand eels. On the East Coast, both species can often be found in salt ponds, bays, and estuaries.

In a few hauls with the seine, Ruth and I had enough silversides for two or three meals. Whitebait is best if eaten the day the fish are caught, but a day or two in the refrigerator before cooking does little harm.

On the beach, keep seined silversides in a bucket, without water, covered with a cloth or seaweed. Rinse them clean of sand and debris in a colander and refrigerate immediately after getting home.

We repeated our successful silverside forays in mid-October and again in early November, although by the latter date most of them had moved into deeper water.

In his book, McClane noted that "whitebait had its origin in England about 1780" and that "the man credited with its invention was a Thames fisherman named Robert Cannon whose heirs assumed the purveying of whitebait, and during the ten-year reign of King George IV they supplied the royal household every day of the season."

He continued, "The esteem in which whitebait was once held is reflected in the annual Ministerial Whitebait Dinner, which some observers believe helped formulate the British Constitution."

The original dish, McClane wrote, "consisted of juvenile herring, sprat, sand lance, smelt, stickleback and pipefish, all being dusted in flour and instantly deep-fried to a crisp succulence."

McClane observed that a whitebait blend of silversides and sand eels "is by most standards the ultimate in flavor." *(November 26, 2005)*

LATE-SUMMER RITUAL:

CRABBING ON THE HUDSON

By James Gorman

WATCH IT, THEY REALLY HURT," my eleven-year-old son said.

"Ouch, it got me!" I replied.

"I told you," he said with a sigh, a resigned look on his face as I shook off the blue crab. Fathers — they never listen.

We were pulling up crab traps in the lower Hudson, pursuing a time-honored late-summer ritual along the river. Visit any pier or dock and you will see people crabbing. Out on the river the commercial crabbers are setting and checking their pots. The crabs are biting, both bait and crabbers.

I tried a couple of different approaches this year. I set a pot in the river and also went out in a boat to get away from other crabbers and try small traps of the sort that open when they hit the bottom. You bait them with something smelly, let them sink to the bottom, and pull them up every so often to see what you have got. As you pull, the trap closes.

There are different reasons to go after crabs. I will take any excuse to get outside on the river. And in a catch-and-release world, crabbing offers something that has largely disappeared from many anglers' lives — the elemental connection to food that you catch yourself.

Just as vegetable gardening introduces the gardener more intimately to the soil and the seasons, crabbing, even for recreation, pulls you more deeply into the life of the river and the movement of tides, and closer to the crabs themselves.

As the wolf in Stephen Sondheim's *Into the Woods* sings about Little Red Riding Hood:

> *There's no possible way*
> *To describe what you feel*
> *When you're talking to your meal*
> *Or when your meal wielding its claws*
> *With unmistakable intent, talks*
> *back to you.*

I do not want to compare myself too closely to Sondheim's wolf, who is bubbling over with predatory sexuality. But there is no mistaking the predatory aspect of crabbing. I even caught my own bait. I could have used squid or frozen fish or chicken necks, all of which can work. But that would not have been as satisfying. So the day before I went crabbing I took my boat to a small tributary of the Hudson and started tossing a small red-and-gold spinner.

One after another, the perch hit the lure. Usually, I throw them back, but this time I kept almost a dozen, some to freeze, some to use right away. I fished in the afternoon on the outgoing tide and planned to start my crabbing the next morning at the beginning of the incoming tide. I was following the advice of a twenty-year-old book on the idea that crabs are probably slow to change their habits, so crabbers might as well follow suit. Crabbing does not seem to change all that quickly.

That afternoon I baited a big overnight crab pot, weighted it down, and set it near some old pilings with an old, well-rinsed detergent bottle for a float. The next morning, right after low tide, my son and I headed out into the river with two small box traps.

First we pulled the big pot and found three crabs, all males. Then we tried a couple of spots with the smaller traps before we hit one that started producing. The rhythm is simple: sit, chat, pull up the trap to see what is in it. Sit, chat, pull. Sit, chat, pull.

It would have been purely idyllic if the chatting did not involve explaining, while rocking gently on small swells, about PCBs in the mud, and why children should not eat anything that comes out of the river, even the silvery striped bass. But my son has heard the story often enough that he practically has the New York Department of Health advisories memorized. (For Hudson River crabs, the recommendation is no more than six per week, and none for children under fifteen and women of childbearing age. You should also discard the cooking liquid and hepatopancreas, or tomalley.)

We left the dock at about eight-thirty and returned a little after ten-thirty with a small catch, eight good-sized males. We let the females and small males go. New York regulations require only that females with eggs attached be released, but the crabbers I talked to let all the females go, so I followed suit.

Sometimes, with some prey, the catching is the big event; the eating is easy. Brook trout, for instance, do not take much cleaning and can be dispatched fairly quickly once they appear on the plate.

With crabs, the catching is only the beginning. If a television nature show were to film humans going after crabs the way they do lions chasing wildebeest, precious little footage would go to the crabbing. The close-ups would all be of the eating, focusing on the unavoidable brutality of killing, dismembering, and ingesting the prey, right up to the final moment when the alpha male (me) tears the cooked crab apart with his hands and sucks the tidbits of flesh from the legs. As this is going on, the rest of the family is making faces about the boiled crab smell in the kitchen.

It may be messy, but there is no mistaking what is going on, and that is one of the things about crabbing that appeal to me. You can kid yourself about a boneless, breaded chicken breast. Who knows where they come from? Vats? Genetic engineering? Birds made completely of soy protein?

But when you eat a crab that you have caught yourself, you know exactly what you are doing, from wiring the dead perch into the trap to trying to crack that claw. It is the sort of experience that either makes you a vegetarian or makes the meat taste all the sweeter.

I guess I am a predator at heart. I thought the crabs I caught were particularly delicious, boiled with melted butter as soon as I took them home, and later as part of a crab salad sandwich on a hamburger bun. I also saved some salad to share with a friend — only six crabs a week, after all.

I am not proselytizing here. Vegetarianism strikes me as an entirely sensible approach to eating, both moral and healthy. But if you are not going to stick to vegetables, it is worth it once in a while to catch, kill, cook, and eat your own prey. It keeps you honest, whether it makes you squeamish or simply hungry, and it brings home, with force, the dangers of pollution.

Still, if you like shellfish, crabs are a good place to start. You do not really want more than six. You do not have to crab in the Hudson; crabs are everywhere. And as to predation, they are invertebrates, so it is not as if you have to go deer hunting.

One word of advice. Watch out for the claws. *(September 8, 2002)*

FAR WATERS

BLUE CHARM

GREEN MACHINE

The New York Times did not assign its "Outdoors" contributors to write about any of the far-flung places covered here. No frantic phone calls were made from an editor, screaming: "They're catching bighead carp in the Ukraine! Get me someone on the next flight to Kiev!"

Instead, some of us who travel on business just happen to slip a pack rod and assorted tackle in our luggage. Others are smart enough to plan vacations around remote rivers and fishing lodges, where the odds of success rise measurably (as does the cost).

Fishing in exotic places brings together a strange mix of the unknown and the familiar. Monkeys hang from trees instead of squirrels. An osprey, with its cosmopolitan range, might fly past looking like a long-lost friend, only to land among a group of flamingos.

Strange languages make basic communication a challenge—a hurdle quickly overcome once rods are strung and the first casts made. After that, anglers can use the universal grunts, groans, and whoops that have worked for millennia. Local customs may be more difficult to navigate, such as failing to cast upstream to a rising trout in Britain, or not drinking copious amounts of Swedish vodka with your plate of fried eels.

If things go well, an exotic fish latches on and is landed. Seeing it for the first time can feel like meeting a celebrity (though fish, unlike most movie stars, look much better in person). If it's a fish you recognize from home but have now caught in a distant land, such as a brown trout in Patagonia, or an Atlantic salmon in Russia, toast your catch with a hearty salúd or nastrovia, for the language barrier has now truly been broken.

WHEN FLY-FISHING IN ENGLAND, PLEASE USE PROTOCOL

By Nicholas Karas

Though the English may have invented fly-fishing and introduced it to Americans during the Revolutionary War, what they practice on their hallowed chalk streams today is a far cry from what most Yanks would consider a serious approach to catching fish.

My introduction to the English way came last summer on the River Itchen, which flows through the eastern edge of the ancient city of Winchester, and the River Test, which parallels the Itchen farther west. The two rivers are England's most famous trout streams, and Winchester and Stockbridge form the heart of fly-fishing in England.

Public fishing as we know it does not exist on England's trout streams. British nobility, affluent farmers or landowners, angler-syndicates, or hotels own all streams and fishing rights. Most are only too happy to lease the right to fish. Costs vary greatly, and range from reasonable to outlandish.

Until a few years ago it was nearly impossible to arrange for a day or two of fishing at a moment's notice on the Test or the Itchen. Enter Orvis, the Vermont-based outdoors outfitter, which bought a beat on the Itchen and two on the Test from Demot Wilson. Wilson also owned The Mill, a fly-fishing shop in Stockbridge, in a building that was registered by William the Conqueror in 1086.

Demands for a beat on English streams in mid-July are not great, so we had no trouble booking the Itchen. Along with the beat comes a ghillie, or guide. On the Abbots Worthy Beat, on the northern outskirts of Winchester, the Itchen varies in width from twenty to thirty feet and moves along steadily, winding and twisting, impeded only by the occasional weir.

As Bill Loader unlocked his ghillie's hut, I absorbed an English pastoral landscape that might have been painted by Gainsborough. The sun, through breaks in the clouds, poured onto the river, onto heavily leafed ash trees on the bank, and onto a scattering of sheep and cattle grazing close to the Itchen's edge.

The land on each side is flat; the valley of the Itchen is broad and the hills are only a hundred or so feet above the floor. The entire region was a tropical limestone shelf that eons ago rose from the ocean. When it rains, water is quickly absorbed through its porous substrata, and only weeks later does it percolate up, cool and clear, to feed the river.

Loader has been a trout fisherman all his life, but only a ghillie for the last decade, since Orvis bought his beat. He wore knee-high Wellingtons; I rented a pair. Americans love to become part of the river and wade into it. But you do not wade into an English chalk stream; you cast from its bank. The Wellingtons keep the heavy dew off your feet.

Then Loader began revealing a litany of fishing protocols foreign to Americans. Only fly-fishing is accepted; preferably dry-fly fishing. If you must use a nymph, it can only be fished downstream. It would be too lethal fished upstream. Seldom are flies larger than a No. 12 used. More often they are 18s and 20s. Larger flies are used only during the mayfly season. I was about to cast when Loader admonished me not to.

"Fishermen here cast only to rising trout," he said. "That

won't be for another hour. Trout here rise like clockwork at eleven each morning. And the rise lasts about an hour."

"What do you do the rest of the time?" I asked.

"You look," he said. "But if one sees finning, you may cast nymphs."

To Englishmen, there is only one real trout: the brown trout. Through a faux pas, rainbow trout were introduced to these streams years ago.

"The American trout is far more aggressive than natives," Loader said. "It reproduces readily and eventually dominates the streams. Caught rainbows are immediately killed. Browns are usually, almost always, returned to the stream.

"There's a finning brace," Loader then pointed out. "You might want to tie on a Gold-Ribbed Hare's-Ear Nymph and give it a go."

I was amazed at how many American fly patterns are used on English streams. Quill Gordons, Hendricksons, and Iron Blue Duns are popular, but the Adams series is the most popular. I was plagued by a wind coming off the sedges on the opposite bank, and while the line made it almost to the fish, the leader and fly were blown back. One bad cast spooked the fish.

While Loader wasn't looking, I replaced the almost weightless nymph with a No. 10 Royal Coachman. Loader immediately noticed and asked what the colorful fly was.

"An English pattern," I answered. "A Royal Coachman."

"I've heard of it," Loader said, "but we don't fish it in England. Maybe a Coachman, but never a Royal Coachman. That is strictly an American modification. It doesn't work here."

About 200 yards upstream, a small feeder entered from the west. Under the opposite bank, I spotted a lone trout finning where the current entered the Itchen. I planted the gaudily colored fly two feet ahead of its snout. The trout shot for it. Before I could take up the slack, it set the hook and made for the feeder.

Feeling the first tension on the fly from the line, the trout bolted into the air. A gorgeously colored rainbow trout, a three-pounder, danced a pirouette, then splashed back and made for the thick ranunculus.

"Keep him out, or for sure he's a goner," Loader said as I tried to lift the trout's head away from the tangling aquatic plant.

I couldn't turn the fish with the 5-weight rod. It dived into the weeds, anchored the hook, and was free.

"Not a very accommodating fish, even to a visiting countryman," Loader said.

It started to drizzle and we took sanctuary under the ancient ash tree. Its trunk was huge, six feet in diameter, and its massive canopy covered the river to the opposite bank. It was just a passing shower; we could see sunshine upriver.

"Your president fished here; Carter was a rather good caster," Loader said. "Just above, I'll show you where he landed a three-pounder."

Loader pointed out places that were sure to hold trout. In just the short distance we had come, his predictions were exacting.

"You get to be that way after eight years on a beat," he said. "It is like having another wife or mistress. At my age, seventy-nine, that's about all I dare manage." *(May 10, 2000)*

FISH STORIES, TOLD

WITH A BROGUE

By Barbara Lloyd

RECESS, IRELAND—A book by the fire at the Lough Inagh Lodge looked ever more enticing than sitting in a boat on a chilly day as the mist outside turned a darker gray. But who among us could resist those fly rods standing so nobly in the back hallway of this County Galway fishing lodge?

"Have you ever fly-fished before?" asked Ronan Creane, the lodge's guide. "Yes," we replied in unison, as couples do. "But not a lot." My husband, Dick Baker, had once cast in the river waters of Oregon and Wyoming, and I had dropped lines from the deep alpine grasses of northwest Montana. But this was a mountain lake on the west coast of Ireland, and we soon found ourselves getting in a boat.

It was a nineteen-foot skiff, a narrow wooden hull that looked like the Rangely guide boats of woodland Maine. One pull of the six-horsepower Yamaha, and we were heading against a freshening breeze along the four-mile lake. Our cache of wet flies—a Bibio, a Black Pennell, and a few Daddy Long Legs—filled an arsenal meant to lure sea trout, brown trout, and Atlantic salmon.

Our guide, a disarmingly self-assured twenty-one-year-old, left no doubt that we would catch something. Creane had just beaten his father, Joe, an international competitor, in a local fishing derby the day before. How he did it was a tale of perseverance that fired up our determination.

Creane, you see, had selected a secluded spot along a nearby lake and waited for the contest to begin. The rules prohibited fishing from a boat as we were allowed to do on Lough Inagh. From the shore instead, our young guide had mounted a daylong fishing vigil. But in the excitement of competition, he had forgotten his rain gear.

Rather than go back to shore for his jacket, Creane kept casting. As his clothes got wetter, he got colder. So he began disrobing; doesn't everyone? He removed his clothing piece by piece. Then he spread his sodden shirt, pants, and underclothing on adjacent bushes, hoping they would dry as the rain began to abate.

No one else was around, which was part of his plan. He was sure he had picked the choicest fishing hole, and was not about to leave it. Not even when it meant fishing in the buff.

At the end of the day, Creane, fully clothed once again, delivered almost nine pounds of fish, a sizable catch that put him in second place in the competition. The winner's total weighed only three more ounces than Creane's. Better yet, our young guide had beaten his father, who finished in third place.

We latched on to the story eagerly as we began our day of fishing. Creane had turned off the boat's engine, and we were drifting down the lake with an oar put out to the side as a rudder. But in less than an hour, dozens of thwarted casts revealed our rookie inadequacies against the fitful breeze. Try as we might, our lines got tangled like used kite string. We hooked everything on the boat but each other, and that was going to be next.

Creane, undoubtedly fearful of being hooked himself, suggested a change of pace. We would troll down the lake with the engine running. Had we been self-respecting fly-fishers, we would have nixed the idea. But we were desperate.

Within minutes, I had the first strike. It was a salmon, albeit a tiny salmon that looked more despondent than I had been. The next catch proved to be a heartier sea trout. Measuring about one pound, it came into the boat with a little kick, not unlike the cutthroat trout I remembered landing several years ago in Montana. We threw my Irish fish back as part of the lake's catch-and-release policy.

It was a whole lot harder to throw back the next one — a two-and-a-quarter-pound brown trout that Creane said was easily the third-largest brown caught on the lake all season. Since we were there in late September, and the fishing year had started in February, I felt a bit smug. But I was not alone. Creane was beside himself with enthusiasm.

"It's a lovely fish," he said excitedly. "To catch a brown that size, the chances are very slim. The biggest fish here this season was 3.2 pounds. Will you send me the photo?"

An hour later, Dick landed a brown that was quite nearly the same size. I could swear it was the same fish. Either way, they were big fish for Lough Inagh, and beautiful. On the way back to shore, I thought I noticed a wistful look on Creane's face.

"I'm very jealous that I didn't catch one of those fish," he said.

I was touched. "I'll send you the pictures," I promised. *(November 28, 1999)*

SALMON AND SEA TROUT IN
REYKJAVIK'S SUBURBS

By John Waldman

NEVER BEFORE COMING to Iceland had I driven through a river. But the evening prior, while on a reconnaissance tour by jeep of the Leirvogsa, the river's warden drove me and the director of Iceland's freshwater fisheries bureau, Arni Isaksson, through a shallow rapids and across tributary streams of this pristine Atlantic salmon river.

Alone, the morning after in my idling rental car, I nervously faced the same gauntlet of feeder streams swamping the poor dirt road that follows the main channel. Donning waders before I attempted the crossing, I gunned the engine and bounded across the clear cobble bottoms of several tributaries and raced toward the first salmon hole of the morning's session.

I hadn't expected to be salmon angling, instead planning on two days of fishing for sea-run brown trout that also enter Iceland's rivers in early autumn to spawn. But when, at the last moment, Arni said I could still purchase a license to fish for salmon for a day on the Leirvogsa, I seized the opportunity.

From my guesthouse in Reykjavik, I could easily see the volcanic dome that towers over the Leirvogsa and which is the tallest mountain on the eastern horizon. However, the Leirvogsa is only a suburban river by Icelandic standards; the Ellidaar flows right through the capital city, producing about 1,500 salmon annually. The Leirvogsa, a smaller river in an almost uninhabited valley, is perhaps a twenty-minute drive from the center of Reykjavik. In the Leirvogsa, about four hundred salmon, mostly grilse, are caught per year.

❖ ❖ ❖

As I neared the first salmon pool, I made a critical mistake, veering a little off the road to avoid a deep-looking puddle. The little Toyota settled on a high spot of turf and wouldn't budge. Solitude is wonderful until you need help; the car was seriously stuck, and I was alone with only scattered Viking horses grazing across the valley. For hours in a cool rain, I alternated between making a few halfhearted casts in the immediate pool and digging the soil from under the car with my hands, a board, and finally a rake and a hay fork that I found in a nearby farmer's shed.

Shortly after noon, I spotted a van near a faraway farmhouse and hiked there to ask for assistance. A somewhat bemused young man and his mother drove me back and noted dryly that I might have been better off to have gone through the puddle. He asked if I intended to catch salmon with farm tools, and then towed the car for free.

With born-again fervor and determined to salvage the day, I headed to the river's fishing cabin, or *veiðhusið*, to take the obligatory midday break. On the way, I passed a deep, fast, flowing chute. Remembering I had seen a salmon jump there the evening before, I stopped and fished, using light spinning gear rather than the overgunned fly rod I had also brought along.

The second cast of a spinner resulted in a fine, lamprey-scarred female grilse, already dark red from having spent weeks in the river following its year at sea. On the next few casts, I lost a sea trout and then landed a larger male salmon that made several of the athletic jumps that have brought the species so much admiration.

At the cabin, I made coffee with river water, ate lunch, and entered my two salmon releases in the river's logbook. The terms of my license required me to relinquish the middle reach of the river in the afternoon. Reasoning that salmon that had been in the Leirvogsa for some time would more likely be far upriver than near the river's mouth, I opted for the upper-most pools.

Upriver, the Leirvogsa's character changed completely. Whereas the middle section flowed at a pleasant pace over a gravel bottom, the headwaters descended in a rush through a gorge — a deep, ragged slash through bedrock. Peering down from promontories, I looked for both fishable pools and sheep trails that could provide access. In many places, sheer vertical walls prevented passage to the next pool, and I was forced to climb back to the top in order to follow the river.

The chasm's bottom was an elemental world of rock and water, patrolled by somber-looking ravens. Choosing between spinning tackle and the fly rod, depending on the pace and flow, I caught two sea trout and two Arctic char, the latter probably lake-run fish from above Trollafoss Falls at the head of the gorge.

While casting in the penultimate pool, I wondered if salmon ascended to the high, terraced plunge basin below the falls. As if in answer, at that moment, a salmon vaulted against the torrent just a few feet away from me. No more salmon struck, but the afternoon passed quickly as I fished and hiked the rugged landscape in a kind of exertive reverie. By dusk I was exhausted, chilled by Iceland's interminable drizzle, and grateful to be only minutes away from a coffee shop and my guesthouse.

The next morning, still charmed by my day on the Leirvogsa, I fished the Varma, a small river a little farther outside of Reykjavik. My party of Robert Darling, a transplanted Londoner, and Derek Mills, a prominent Scottish salmonid biologist and writer, leapfrogged down the river from pool to pool.

The Varma was brimming with bright sea trout — transformed to silver by their marine existence but still sporting the dark spots of their river kin. The sea trout, glorious leapers with the spirit, if not the size, of salmon, were holding deep and responded well to weighted wet flies. Derek put on a clinic, taking six sea trout and a large resident brown in the brief morning session before he had to return to the city, where he planned to take the largest sea trout to a smokehouse.

Geothermal springs vented towers of steam in the distance, and sheep loitered on the riverbanks, but I focused on the flow, taking sea runs, browns, and small rainbow trout escapees from a fish farm, and even a salmon smolt. I had planned to leave with Robert in midafternoon, but I elected to stay until nightfall and then make a long walk back to a depot for a bus to Reykjavik, powerless to leave such a generous river. *(October 23, 1996)*

PASS THE EEL, PASS THE VODKA,

AND CARRY ON A TRADITION

BY JAMES PROSEK

I REALLY LIKE this fellow, Hansa the eel fisher," my host Magnus Bolmstrand told me in a measured tone the night I arrived at his home in Åhus, Sweden. "He is one of my favorite people. He is what I call *naturkraft*."

I asked Magnus what *naturkraft* meant.

"It's a kind of nature power," he said. "Hansa gets his power from being in nature, and then bestows that power on the people around him."

In a sleepy region of southeast Sweden called Skåne, there are three major emblems of culture: apples, wheat for vodka, and eels. In many places the wheatfields and orchards stretch to the Baltic Sea and a sandy beach shaped like a crescent moon sixty miles long, called the Alakust, or the eel coast.

Eels are not only eaten there, but also revered as a quasi-mythical creature. In Brantevik, near the Viking ruin called Ales Stenar, there is rumored to be an eel in a well that is over a century old, placed by a resident who recorded the event in his diary in 1850.

On the coast are old cottages, buried in the sand by storms so that they look like A-frames. They have been the homes of eel fishermen for more than three hundred years, standing on the beach and marking the territory in the sea that has been handed down since the region of Skåne (pronounced SKOH-na) was won from the Danes in 1658 in the Roskilde Peace. The generals who helped the Swedish nobility conquer the land were given the fishing rights, out to 600 meters off shore. It is the only place in Sweden where you can own property in the sea.

The southeast coast is special because it is along this beach that the adult eels, after spending eight to twenty-five years in freshwater lakes and rivers, make their way from Finland, Russia, and Sweden, swimming through the Baltic and the Denmark Strait, to the Atlantic and, famously, to the Sargasso Sea to spawn.

Hansa, or Hans Inge Olofsson, an eel fisherman at the cottage called Rumpabowden, often contemplates this mystery as he pulls his boat off the beach into the surf to collect his nets. He has been fishing for eels here for twenty years, as his father and his grandfather did.

The fishing rights have been leased by the fishermen since they were acquired in the conquest, and the payment from the fishermen to the landowners was in eels, a coveted fatty food fish in Scandinavia. It was also stipulated that in exchange for the fishing rights, the fisherman would throw a party for the owner and his friends, sometimes for more than a hundred people. These events, called an *alagille*, or eel party, were the reason I went to Sweden last August.

Traditionally, the party was for men only. In fact, if a woman was spotted in the morning by an eel fisherman on his way to go fishing, he would turn around and go home. Not only because he believed he would not catch anything, but also because he thought his life was in danger. Although the nets are usually not more than a quarter-mile offshore, the storms in the Baltic can come fast, and the water is frigid. There are many superstitions, and many stories of eel fishermen who never made it home.

The parties begin in late August as the eels begin making their spawning migrations and, as long as the catch is good, run all winter. These days the parties are smaller, twelve to twenty people, and are attended by men and women.

At an *alagille*, eel is cooked six or more different ways: in soup, fried, grilled over linden wood, boiled, baked, or smoked. The first man to eat enough eel so that he lines the perimeter of his plate with eel spines is declared the eel king. Hansa said, pointing to a bottle of aquavit, that the sign of a successful eel party is when you do not remember anything the next day.

Within sight of Hansa's nets, which we pulled one morning at first light, is the town of Åhus (pronounced OH-hoos), where a tower marks the state-run plant that produces every bottle of Absolut vodka. The vodka, Hansa says, helps the eel go down.

These fish are prepared to make a journey of several thousand miles, and are solid balls of fat. It is not easy to try one piece of the six different preparations at a traditional *alagille*.

After spending a week with Hansa, who tailors Beach Boys songs to his own lyrics and sings them while fishing, I was asked to participate in an *alagille*. He no longer prepares the dinners; these are done by his wife, an artist named Maria Brombarg, and their daughter Anna. I was careful, after a warning from Magnus, to try only a little of each dish so I would not be too full for apple pie made with native Skåne apples.

I drank all that was offered, because I believed the myth that the alcohol cut the fat and allowed you to eat more eel. And I suppose I attended a successful eel party, because I don't remember much — except a dark room lighted with candles and Hansa playing his guitar and singing and laughing.

The eel is among the most resilient of animals, and one of

the hardest to kill. At 5:00 a.m., as I lay in bed, it felt as if the pieces of eel I had eaten were assembling in my stomach and were trying to make an escape up my esophagus, determined to reach their place of spawning in the wide Sargasso. *(February 22, 2004)*

A WEEK OF HIGHS AND LOWS

AT THE END OF THE EARTH

By Peter Kaminsky

THE WEATHER IN Russia's Kola Peninsula, home to the world's greatest salmon run, can turn on a kopeck. So can the fishing. In a week on the Pana River, a two-hour helicopter flight from Murmansk, I had fishing for Atlantic salmon straight out of a daydream and, right alongside, rotten luck that had me questioning my karma.

It started out gangbusters. Four salmon, up to ten pounds, in the first hour and one for my guide, Vassily Vassilyvich. By the standards of Scotland or Canada, it was already a productive week's total.

But nature is capricious: those fish would be the last that I caught for two days. The annual spawning run had already peaked. Still, there were fish to be caught.

My hopes for the Pana were so high because I had been reading about the bounteous catches on the Kola ever since the 1980s, when American and English outfitters had first discovered that the warm waters of the Gulf Stream, which made for good salmon fishing in the north of Norway and Finland, also carried eastward to the Kola. There the combination of inaccessibility and fertile waters had produced Atlantic salmon runs of prehistoric proportions.

But, as with all else in angling, it is always a question of right place, right time. We only had half of it right (the place). I sank into a slough of despond. I cast and cast, my two-handed rod awakening pain in muscles that I was previously ignorant of owning.

Vassily returned to the run where we had had luck on our first morning. I cast into the chute favored by salmon, lifted my line, and cast again. Just then I was buffeted by a freak gust that presaged the arrival of a hailstorm. The fly took on a will of its own and somehow, even though I was casting from my right side, it found a way to lodge itself about an eighth of an inch from my left eye.

Providentially, Justin McCarthy, the chief guide for our outfitters, Roxton Bailey Robinson, was in camp and he arrived to assure me that he could have it out lickety-split. We putt-putted back to the lodge, where, after I threw down two shots of a rare single malt and spent fifteen minutes with an ice pack on my eye, Justin performed the textbook (though counterintuitive) operation of pressing down on the eye of the hook and yanking it out with a loop of monofilament. Mirabile dictu, it did not hurt as much as a mosquito bite.

I was eager to fish, and asked McCarthy if he was game to return to the slick tail of a pool where we had seen a few salmon. The wind lay down, and the afternoon light fell in golden shafts through the spruce forest. The bankside verge was carpeted with an uncountable variety of wildflowers, taking advantage of the short Arctic summer and constant daylight: globe flowers like small yellow peonies, lacy Labrador tea, and the miniature purple bell shapes of the lovely if unattractively named goat vetch.

A salmon jumped. "Forget him," Justin advised. "He's running upstream."

Instead my guide directed me to cast in front of a rock that was a favorite salmon lie. A downstream mend configured my line into a shallow parabola that allowed the fly, a Blue

Charm, to swim across the current at a salmon-summoning speed.

Tap-tap, then the scream of the reel and a tail-walking, head-shaking fight with an eight-pound fish. I felt lucky again.

Next morning, Freddie Elwes, our principal outfitter, had sent out an all-points bulletin that was answered by the offer of a helicopter ride to a well-oxygenated riffle where some of the Russian guides were sure there would be a concentration of salmon.

On cue, a Russian Mi-8, looking like nothing so much as an airborne edition of those 1953 Chevrolets that cruise the Malecón in Havana, picked us up for the fifty-mile trip down the Pana and Varzuga Rivers. Accompanying us was Svet Mihailovich (it was his helicopter), a fellow of ursine proportions with a luxuriant gray mustache and a camouflage outfit.

We touched down at a long riffle known as Arihleka. No sooner had we entered the surging stream than a salmon leaped. Then another, and another. Bright salmon still on the run upstream.

Freddie, an expert salmon angler, talked me through all the eddies and microcurrents, and within five minutes I was fast to a fish. I looked downstream. So did my longtime fishing buddy Josh Feigenbaum. The salmon went through their whole repertoire of leaping, thrashing, making a commotion, head-shaking, leaping some more, rushing away each time they saw the net. But eventually we landed both fish.

And so the morning went, and by 1:00 p.m. I had caught a half dozen up to eleven pounds. We stopped for lunch, a streamside grill of fresh salmon with onion, dill, salt, pepper, garlic, and lemon, wrapped in foil and thrown on the coals for five minutes a side. Afterward, my pungent cigar kept the gnats and mosquitoes at bay.

Then into the river again. In that whole day, I never covered more than seventy-five yards of stream. When the helicopter once again hovered into view, I had landed a dozen Atlantics, and all members of our party reported similar totals. Four anglers, forty-five salmon. I felt very lucky to be alive in a time when — at the ends of the Earth — such wild creatures still teem as they have since humankind first appeared. *(July 8, 2002)*

FISHING AMONG THE
FALKLANDS' SHIPWRECKS

By Stephen Sautner

OST PEOPLE CONSIDER 1982 the most sig-
nificant date in Falkland Islands history.
Twenty years ago this month, the world be-
came aware of this isolated archipelago in the South Atlantic
when a short but bloody war erupted over Argentina's attempt
to reclaim what it calls Islas Malvinas from the British, a con-
flict that stemmed from a series of disputed territorial claims
dating from the early eighteenth century.

From an angling perspective, however, the banner year is
1940, when fertile brown trout eggs from Chile were planted
in a handful of rivers and estuaries. Several subsequent intro-
ductions over the years resulted in strong runs of sea-run
browns throughout many of the Falklands' waterways.

In fact, most British consider the sea trout fishing in the
Falklands to be far better than at home, where these world-
class gamefish are pursued with obsession. Indeed, the twenty-
two-plus-pound monster taken here in 1992 stands a full two
ounces larger than the current British record.

Filled with thoughts of leg-sized browns, I wound through
the narrow streets of the capital, Stanley (population, 1,750),
in a taxi, clutching a tube that contained a four-piece, 8-weight
fly rod. Next to me, my backpack was stuffed with a pair of
chest waders, a fly reel, a map, and a single fly box filled with
streamers and wet flies.

Destination: Moody Brook, which, according to Peter Lapsley's excellent handbook *Fishing for Falklands Sea Trout* (Falkland Islands Tourist Board), probably received the first shipment of trout eggs. According to my map, it was also the closest river to town, some three miles from my hotel room.

❖   ❖   ❖

As we drove along, the Falklands' rich maritime history practically screamed out at every turn. The skeletons of several wrecked sailing ships could be seen listing on distant mudflats, their wooden sides bleached almost white after more than a century of sun, salt, and wind. On a gentle hill that overlooked town, proud crews from another era had spelled out the names of famous ships with rocks to commemorate their visit. Among them were Charles Darwin's *Beagle*, and Sir Ernest Shackleton's *Endurance*, whose ill-fated attempt to cross Antarctica may be the greatest true-life adventure story of the twentieth century.

Eventually we came to where the harbor narrowed, and Moody Brook gently flowed under a small bridge and emptied into saltwater. At first glance it looked pitifully small, the size of a native brook trout stream — minus the brookies and hemlocks.

After the driver dropped me off, I found myself alone, except for an elderly gentleman who was cutting peat in a nearby field. I strolled over to him and asked about the fishing.

"No fish in here," he told me in a rather stern British accent. "Too small. Try the Murrell River, over that ridge." He pointed to a rolling hill studded with rocky outcrops.

"How far is it?" I asked.

"Another two miles," he said. "Just walk north. When you get there, head downstream. And don't go past the fence."

"Private property?" I asked.

"Minefield," he said. He glanced at my rod tube and backpack. "Trout fishing?" he said.

"Yep," I said.

"There's mullet there, too," he said. "Best bait's a piece of mutton."

I thanked him and headed north.

When I reached the top of the hill, I saw one last reminder of the Falklands War: a bomb crater, thirty feet across and still black and lifeless. (I would later find out that I had crossed Wireless Ridge, the scene of one of the war's more famous battles.) As I made my way down the other side of the ridge, all signs of civilization dropped behind me, replaced by gently rolling hills covered in an endless sea of diddle-dee, a heather-like grass that is to the Falklands what sagebrush is to Wyoming. In the distance, the Murrell River shimmered in the afternoon light.

When I finally reached the water, the tide had just begun to flood. The river itself looked featureless, except for a sub-merged sandbar that dropped off into a deep hole in front of me. With a pair of upland geese staring, I took off my hiking boots, slipped on my waders, and began assembling my tackle. I tied on a white Deceiver, a universal saltwater fly, then waded into the river and stripped off several arm-lengths of line.

Making the first cast into new water — particularly when it is more than 6,000 miles from home — always feels some-what daunting, like reading the first sentence of a 600-page novel. What if I'm wasting my time? What if it's awful? What if I should have brought mutton?

I double-hauled and shot the fly fifty feet into the river, then began a slow, stripping retrieve. The Deceiver twitched and danced just under the surface like a wounded baitfish. To my amazement, a large boil appeared behind the fly almost immediately.

I continued retrieving, bracing my shoulders in anticipa-tion of the strike. But it never happened. Whatever fish had tracked the fly apparently wasn't fooled enough to eat it.

After a few more casts, I made my way down the shoreline. I tied on a black-and-purple Zonker, thinking that perhaps a darker fly would do the trick. It worked. A fish thumped it on the first cast, hooking itself solidly, then dashed off, peeling line and shaking its head all the way.

I held the rod high and let the fish run. When it stopped, I pumped the rod and gobbled up line. The fish then rolled a few feet away, showing off dark charcoal sides and a broad, flat head. Clearly this was no sea trout. A few seconds later I managed to slide ashore a Falklands mullet of about three pounds. Actually a species of rock cod, the mullet has the underslung mouth and broad tail of a redfish, the head and coloring of a cobia, and the graceful pectoral fins of a jack crevalle. Reportedly they reach twenty pounds.

I popped the Zonker out of the mullet's mouth and slid it back into the river, where it quickly swam off, pushing a small wake. The tide continued to flood. Small eddies began swirling along a rocky shoreline just downriver. Not knowing what good sea-trout water might look like, the spot seemed as good as any. When I reached it, I switched back to the Deceiver and resumed my casting-and-twitching routine.

After a few casts, something grabbed the fly with a rush and immediately hurled itself from the river in a wild leap. It was my first sea-run brown trout, though it looked to be a good twenty pounds lighter than the current Falklands record. Still, the fish went through a full repertoire of tail-walks, spirited runs, and head-shakes.

Eventually, I slid my hand underneath a plump eighteen-incher, with chrome sides peppered with large, jagged spots. Falklands sea trout are said to average two to four pounds, but most regulars will tell you that ten-pounders are not that uncommon. I could only imagine the fight from such a fish.

I gently released it and continued to work my way down the shoreline. Another fish took hard, then made four jumps in nearly as many seconds. Another eighteen-incher came to my hand and was quickly released.

Over the next hour, I landed two smaller fish and lost another four before the action slowed. Apparently a small school of trout had briefly stationed itself in front of me, then headed upriver with the tide. The Murrell River, lifeless-looking two hours ago, had just revealed one of its secrets.

But the realization of a five-mile hike back to town began to sink in. Reluctantly, I waded ashore, replaced my waders with hiking boots, and stuffed my backpack with the rest of my tackle. With the sun sliding toward the horizon, I began the long walk across the diddle-dee, over Wireless Ridge, past ancient shipwrecks, to my hotel room in Stanley. *(April 7, 2002)*

WHERE TROUT ARE BIGGER THAN THE TALLEST OF TALES

By Peter Kaminsky

O URS IS AN era in which there is not much fishing that is as good as it used to be, and even less that is better than it ever was.

The Rio Grande on the island of Tierra del Fuego, off the southern tip of South America, is a happy anomaly. Over the last thirty years the river has produced sea-run brown trout in steadily increasing sizes. According to Mel Krieger, the West Coast writer and fly-fishing evangelist, who recently introduced me to this stream, "The Rio Grande, right now, is the greatest anadromous fishery on earth."

Big statement, but then, so are the trout. In six days of fishing at the sprawling Estancia Maria Behety, in bone-chilling water and tooth-rattling wind, I landed a half-dozen trout over fifteen pounds and one weighing twenty-seven and a half pounds on a No. 12 Prince Nymph, the piscatorial equivalent, I suppose, of shooting a grizzly with a slingshot. My accomplishments were just about average for our group of fourteen anglers.

Why are the trout so big? There is probably a combination of factors: a strict catch-and-release policy over the length of the river; no commercial fishing or netting where the Rio Grande begins in the Atlantic; the tendency of species to achieve their largest sizes at the extremities of their range; and, Krieger says, a warming of the Antarctic waters that has enriched the whole food chain.

❖   ❖   ❖

I arrived late last month, braced for the legendary winds that whip across the Patagonian steppe. Providentially, the winds were usually no worse than a gusty October afternoon at Montauk. An 8-weight rod more than did the job.

At twilight on March 28, I spent an hour that I now remember more fully than I can recall some years. A morning session had yielded a couple of ten-pounders and a few airborne leaps for freedom by considerably larger fish that spit, straightened, or broke my hooks.

That afternoon we went to a stretch of river where a short cast into a deep pool was supposed to summon a leviathan. But the water was cold and the fish sluggish. My partner, Mickey Schwartz of El Paso, and our guide, Alberto Molina Gomez, were stymied.

Maybe it was the fearsome aspect of Schwartz's hat that put the trout down. It was a towering Alaskan fur headpiece, reminiscent of Cossack battle gear. Gomez's more likely explanation was that the lack of a current left our flies looking lifeless and unappetizing.

At seven o'clock my inner fisherman told me, *Forget it, pal.*

But Gomez, perhaps the most experienced and knowledgeable guide on the river, was determined.

"Vamos al otro pozo," he said. Let's go to another pool.

I hesitated. "Alberto, it's seven o'clock. We quit at eight. Fifteen minutes to get there doesn't leave us much time to fish. But you're the guide."

The sun descended, the sky turned a brazen crimson behind the mountains of Chile. Melting snows from a late-season storm brought the water temperature down to 38 degrees.

We pulled up to a bend in the river. *"Acá,"* Gomez announced. Right about here.

As with salmon, Rio Grande trout, returning to spawn,

often stop at predictable spots, sometimes no bigger than a living room.

"Take the downstream bend," Schwartz offered in his courtly West Texas drawl.

I tied on a No. 12 Prince Nymph, best described as a combination Zug Bug and classic Catskills wet fly. A fish rolled, reminiscent of the porpoising motion of a rolling tarpon. It is a seductive display, but rarely does it result in a take.

I ignored it and quarter-cast downstream, throwing in an upstream mend to give the 200-grain sink tip time to carry the fly to the bottom, where the trout would surely be, if they were anywhere. The rod pointed straight at the moon, full and orange as it rose over the bank. A flock of banduria ibises, whose call is a cheering combination of a stutter and a giggle, flew over me. For two weeks their evening flights heralded a few moments of good fishing.

The fly stopped and the line became taut. I pulled back. "Bottom," I told myself, thinking that I had hung up on a champa, a caved-in grassy bank.

But then the bottom moved. It gave two jolting thumps. I reeled up. The fish took line: first my shooting head, then my running line, then my backing. I followed along the riverbank, trying to stay even with the fish. In counterpoint to my frenzy, the trout shook its head with a percussive snap.

My rod tip bowed. Then it recovered, slowly. Over and over. Every now and then the fish burst for the cover of the far bank. I countered by moving my rod tip. My wrist ached, my fingers began to seize up in the gathering darkness and deepening cold.

"*Tranquilo,*" Gomez counseled, which roughly translates to "Easy, boy."

I backed away from the stream, slowly and with a light tread, like someone easing out of a room so as not to wake a sleeping baby. Luck was with me. The trout came to the surface. Gomez dipped his net and captured the fish. In the moonlight I could see it was bright silver, a recent returnee from the ocean, full of vigor and fight.

He took out his scale. Twelve and a half kilos.

I did the math: twenty-seven and a half pounds, its length nearly thirty inches.

On any other stream, if I caught a fish that was thirty inches long, it would make my year.

Gomez revived it in the current for a minute. He let go of its tail. The huge trout disappeared into the deep, dark water: slowly, like a silver ghost melting back into the night, as the memory of it took up permanent residence in my soul. *(April 21, 2002)*

FISHING INTO THE TEETH
OF THE AMAZON

By Stephen Sautner

TEFÉ, BRAZIL — Having just one hour to fish the Amazon Basin is a little like setting out to climb Mount Everest in shorts and a T-shirt: failure is virtually guaranteed. But sixty minutes is all Jim Barborak and I had to ply this largest of all river systems, with a dozen tributaries larger than the Mississippi.

An ecologist with the Wildlife Conservation Society, Barborak had just completed a meeting at the Mamirauá Sustainable Development Reserve, in the heart of Brazil's seasonally flooded forest, where pink dolphins swim beneath trees filled with squirrel monkeys and toucans. He and his colleagues had outlined plans to further protect this surreal landscape. Now it was time to go fishing.

At exactly fifty-nine minutes before a potbellied riverboat would take the entire group to the small city of Tefé outside the reserve, Barborak and I loaded our gear hastily into a small wooden launch. Our orders from the group were strict: be back on time or swim home.

So we raced upriver, with Barborak chatting away with our two guides in broken Portuguese over the roar of the outboard. Behind us, dolphins rolled in our wake, flashing dorsal fins the color of a baby's bottom. High in a tree, a tangle of arms and legs turned out to be an upside-down sloth that looked as if it had not moved in weeks.

When we eventually slowed down, Barborak turned and said, "We're fishing for piranha." Then the guide cut the motor and eased into a narrow channel flowing into the jungle.

We glided in silently as trees and vines closed around us. The otherwise blistering heat seemed to drop a few degrees, though the humidity felt as steamy as ever. A troop of howler monkeys could be heard in the distance, their raspy, breathy calls somehow sounding like the ocean heard through a seashell.

Barborak immediately began casting a spinner. I chose the local tackle: a long cane pole rigged with a plain hook that looked straight out of Huck Finn — except for the wire leader to ward off the piranha's teeth. The two guides and I baited up and lowered our rigs into the muddy water. Just before their lines settled, each guide suddenly thrashed his rod tip, violently churning the river's surface.

Barborak and I looked at each other quizzically. He then began speaking to the guides in Portuguese, then nodding and laughing as they replied.

"It attracts the piranha," he said, casting again. "It sounds like something that fell out of a tree."

So I, too, slapped the water hard, trying my best to imitate a hapless sloth or squirrel monkey.

A few minutes later, one guide yanked a brilliant red-bellied piranha the size of an average bluegill into the boat. The second guide did the same, followed by Barborak, who landed one on his spinner. I remained fishless, despite flogging the water to a froth. We briefly admired the fierce-looking fish, doing the requisite dental exam of their amazing teeth, before tossing them back.

With the clock ticking away, we cast and slapped and churned away at the mighty Amazon, with Barborak and the guides releasing a few more piranha. Then a much larger fish boiled a few yards away, showering a school of baitfish.

"*Tucunaré,*" one guide said to the other.

In my vocabulary of a half dozen Portuguese words, including those for *please, bathroom,* and *beer, tucunaré* is one I committed to memory. It is the name for peacock bass, a large, spectacularly colored gamefish known for surface strikes that would humble the meanest bluefish.

Barborak began casting to where the *tucunaré* had boiled. I quickly grabbed the heavy spinning outfit I had stowed and tied on a favorite swimming plug I use for striped bass. Just before I cast, I showed it to one of the guides, who smiled in approval.

The lure splashed down next to a mat of floating grass, and I began twitching it back. Almost immediately, something banged the lure, flashing silver and leaving a good-sized swirl. But somehow it missed the two sets of treble hooks.

The next few casts went fishless. Then a piranha slashed at the plug's head and cut the line. When the guide saw the plug drifting away, he eased the boat into the current, scooped it up, and handed it back to me. I thanked him in Portuguese, proudly using one of the six words.

"Time's up," Barborak announced, glaring at his watch and shaking his head in disappointment. A few miles away, the riverboat would be arriving soon. So I handed the guide my plug, gesturing that it now belonged to him. He looked confused for a moment, then grinned and took it from me.

I pictured him returning the next day, having jury-rigged the plug to the cane pole, then slapping it beneath the trees, where a giant peacock bass would be waiting. "*Tucunaré,*" he said, pointing to the water. We both nodded knowingly, two fishermen now speaking in the clearest of terms. *(May 24, 2004)*

IN REMOTE NORTH OF CANADA,
IT'S A PIKE-EAT-PIKE EXISTENCE

By Ken Schultz

S ELWYN LAKE, SASKATCHEWAN — Bruce Holt must have been reading my mind as we both stood on the spruce-lined shore of Selwyn Lake, devouring the last pieces of tender, sweet fish that the native guide William Robillard had cooked on an open fire.

"Pretty hard to beat this," Holt said. He was referring to the delicious lunch, the main entrée of which had been finning nearby just an hour earlier, as well as to the beautiful wilderness of northern Canada's sixtieth parallel and to all the northern pike we'd caught in the first three and a half hours of this fishing adventure.

Five hours earlier we had been at Stony Rapids, a hamlet with a large population of Dene Indians, from which a floatplane had ferried us to the rustic five-year-old lodge at Selwyn Lake. Outside the air terminal in Stony Rapids, a weathered hand-painted sign depicting an angler fighting a large fish proclaimed this region "Last of the Great Northern Fishing in Saskatchewan."

"Last" undoubtedly meant provincial northernmost, and "great" was no understatement if the results of our morning effort were a true indication.

There is nothing like starting off an angling adventure with slam-bang action, and the two of us had probably caught and released two dozen pike, some as large as fifteen pounds, even doing battle within shouting distance of the lunch site, the smell of the campfire wafting by as the fishing rod strained to subdue another feisty battler.

Notoriously aggressive, northern pike are a special attraction for anglers who love to cast and retrieve lures or flies. They are often found in ultraclear and super-shallow water, and can often be sighted for precise casting, somewhat like stalking prime flats species in saltwater.

We'd had success with a host of lures and flies, and three times had both hooked pike simultaneously. Often the fish had followed and abruptly struck in a startling fashion close to the boat.

❖   ❖   ❖

With lunch over, we decided to try something completely different, and began casting surface lures. Holt, who had had great success using large streamer flies on a fly rod, was on the verge of trying a fly-rod popper when the big plug he was using, a double-propellered surface version that was retrieved in a noisy ripping fashion, disappeared in an explosion.

He caught the pike, about a ten-pounder, which caused Robillard to suggest I fish with a gaudy chartreuse buzzbait. A lure normally reserved for largemouth bass, the buzzbait churns across the surface in a manner not unlike a paddling duckling. My heartbeat spiked the first time a pike suddenly struck, and we were into yet another spree of fish-catching.

Some 600 miles north of Saskatoon and straddling the Saskatchewan–Northwest Territories border, Selwyn is forty-five miles long, seventeen miles wide, and packed with islands and treacherous reefs. A forty-minute trip by floatplane from Stony Rapids, it is not only full of pike, but loaded with lake trout, some of which top thirty pounds. Moose, bear, wolves, and caribou range here, and the call of loons is a common occurrence.

The only full-scale facility to be found on the shores of the lake, Selwyn Lake Lodge was built just five years ago, and anglers now come from all over North America. With the exception of one or two kept for daily shore lunch, all fish are released.

It was late afternoon when one of those events that anglers talk about for years occurred. I had hooked a small pike on a bright, shallow-running plug. The fish came toward me and was about ten feet from the boat when a large pike suddenly appeared like a cruise missile homing on its target. Just as the smaller pike was at the side of the boat, it turned sideways and the jaw of the big pike opened cavernously and clamped completely over the smaller fish behind its gills.

Robillard yelled and grabbed his landing net. The pike streaked a short distance away, so I put the reel in free-spool temporarily to avoid pulling on the hooked smaller fish and perhaps yanking it out of the mouth of the big pike, which now turned and swam toward the boat as Robillard lunged unsuccessfully with the net.

"Too big," he said. "I can't get it."

Indeed, it looked sort of like a hammerhead-shaped creature, with the smaller pike crosswise in the mouth of the bigger fish. The duo disappeared under the boat and emerged near the bow, swimming away, the big pike seemingly oblivious to the fact that its lunch was tethered to my rod. I applied moderate rod pressure on the fish, and it came again for the boat.

Then, in a blur of frantic madness—which we could not fathom later—the captor released its victim, which, perhaps simultaneously, became free of the lure, and the big pike became hooked in the mouth by the front single hook of the plug. It streaked off for a short distance, turned for the boat for a third time, and as it rushed toward us I leaned hard on the rod and lifted the fish's head up so it swam deep in the waiting landing net, which Robillard quickly lifted into the boat in a hail of splashing water and writhing fish.

Forty-one inches long and estimated by William at between eighteen and twenty pounds, it was a trophy-caliber pike. When released, it streaked off, probably to catch up with its lunch again. *(April 11, 2000)*

STANDING ON A MOUNTAINTOP, CASTING FOR BONEFISH

BY STEPHEN SAUTNER

GLOVER'S REEF MARINE RESERVE, BELIZE —
It felt strange traveling thirty miles offshore, across
a deep, featureless trench in the Caribbean known
simply as The Blue, just so I could cast a fly into eight inches
of water. But to reach the shallow tidal flats of this pristine marine wilderness, one has to venture beyond the continental
shelf to a submerged mountain range whose peaks make up
the richest coral atoll in the Western Hemisphere.

Dead center along Glover's Reef lies Middle Key, a four-
teen-acre island of swaying coconut palms straight out of *Gilli-
gan's Island*. On this tiny key stands an active research station
run by the Wildlife Conservation Society where visiting scientists study everything from spawning Nassau grouper to huge
spiny lobsters that die of old age in Glover's protected waters.

Here is also where Todd Duncan, the research station's
manager, told me about the schools of bonefish that feed on
the flats just off his front porch. During the ninety-minute
boat ride from the mainland, Duncan gave me a crash course
on the finer points of bonefishing. Use a fly that matches the
color of the bottom, he said over the roar of twin outboard mo-
tors. If a fish shows interest, pause your retrieve so it can catch
up and eat it. Lastly, when a bonefish runs, let it go.

For that last point, I needed no coaching. With an oversized forked tail that propels a sleek, bullet-shaped body

capable of thirty-mile-an-hour sprints, the diminutive bonefish (a ten-pounder is a monster) has caused some of the best anglers of the last century to gush with praise. Zane Grey called fishing for them "the strangest and most thrilling, the lonesomest and most all-satisfying of all kinds of angling." Van Campen Heilner, who traveled the world casting for everything from brook trout to swordfish, elegantly wrote in 1937, "From my personal experience he is the gamest fish for which I ever wet a line."

When we docked at Middle Key, Duncan had to give a tour to a group of visiting scientists, but not before pointing me to a small flat dotted with patches of coral and swaying turtle grass. I quickly strung up my rod and splashed through bathtub-warm, ankle-deep water. With each step, all manner of crabs and juvenile fish scuttled and darted in every direction. A bit of bottom broke off and swam away in the form of a bizarre yellow flounder. A spooked needlefish dived headlong into a school of glass minnows, which in turn showered in a burst of silver spray. Meanwhile, just a few hundred yards from where I stood, on the far side of the exposed reef crest, the bottom plummeted to an amazing mile and a half deep.

Almost immediately I spied pointed tails poking above the surface of the flat just a long cast away. Bonefish. Some swam in small groups of up to a dozen. Periodically the school would rush forward, probably to fight over some hapless shrimp they cornered in the turtle grass. Other fish swam alone, cruising leisurely as if on some sort of aquatic stroll.

It seemed almost too easy, with so many fish obviously feeding in front of me. But after half an hour of near misses and outright blunders, I realized that I was fishing in saltwater's equivalent of a limestone spring creek. One pod of bonefish had gathered around my shrimp pattern, then bolted away in apparent horror. Another one had actually followed the fly for several yards, pushing a small wake in less than a foot of water. But the fish kept coming. I crouched as low as I could, but it saw my profile, then veered off to parts unknown. Duncan's rule of stopping the fly so the fish can catch up flashed in my mind like a forgotten passage of the Bible.

A midday squall had begun to gather on the horizon, sending gray curtains of rain over some nameless key far in the distance. The sound of the surf breaking on the reef crest hung in the humid air. Just then, another tailing bonefish meandered down the flat, slowly paralleling me. Like others before it, the fish seemed to mosey rather than swim, quietly making its way along the edge of a turtle grass bed. When it turned and headed in my direction, I crouched down, false-cast, then dropped the fly five feet in front of it.

When the fish got within two feet of the fly, I twitched the line gently, making the drab olive pattern jump from the grass like a fleeing shrimp. The bonefish immediately responded, closing within inches. I let the fly pause. Then the fish's entire upper tail broke the surface, waving like a flag signaling victory. I tightened the line and felt a satisfying weight — followed by absolute mayhem.

Despite twenty years of reading about a bonefish's initial burst of speed, nothing could have prepared me for that first run. Line immediately yanked from my hand, flew through the guides of my rod, then poured off my reel in a blur. The fish became some haywire torpedo sending a wake blasting across the flat, and spooking what seemed like every other bonefish in Belize. I desperately held the rod over my head, trying to keep the line from catching on bits of coral.

The bonefish stopped briefly, only to take off again in a wide arc, allowing me to gain a few turns of line. I tried to pump it in closer, but it unleashed another powerful run, albeit slightly less intense than the first. But by its third and fourth attempts, it was down to taking just a few yards of line with each run-off. A few minutes after that, a three-pound bonefish lay in my hands, exhausted.

Its silvery sides felt surprisingly hard, as if they were forged from some secret high-tech alloy, and its large eyes gave it a perpetually worried look. All the while its oversized forked tail twitched, searching for water to slice through. I removed the fly and opened my hands. The bonefish dashed away, leaving me alone in calf-deep water, standing on the summit of a mountain. *(December 28, 2003)*

IN UKRAINE, EXPLORING
THE RICHES OF THE DNIEPER

By John Waldman

JUDGING FROM MY first look at the Dnieper River in Kiev, Ukraine's great city exists mainly as a base camp for anglers. The river's deeper holes were being fished by anglers in a motley armada of mostly anti-quated rowboats, canoes, and rafts. Along the shores, fisher-men cast from beaches, rickety stands, and even stepladders placed in the shallows.

That it was a weekday did not quell the fishing hordes; unfortunately, Ukraine's depressed and uncertain economy makes the river highly attractive to the area's unemployed as a source of food and, if luck allows, maybe enough fish to sell for a few extra kopecks.

The Dnieper is to Ukraine what the Mississippi is to the United States, a broad river of enormous recreational, com-mercial, and cultural significance, coursing through its heart-land. And, like the Mississippi, the Dnieper has been overly domesticated by a series of dams and locks, with Kiev situated on a riverine portion of the immense Kanev Reservoir, the next body of water downriver from the ruins of the Chernobyl nuclear station.

I had been invited to Ukraine, with several colleagues, to assess the state of fisheries in the Kanev Reservoir and the Dnieper estuary. Our hosts, from the Ministry of Fisheries of Ukraine, had welcomed my group with unbridled hospitality, each of our many work meetings ending with a feast: black sturgeon caviar, fish stews and soups, fried and smoked fishes, produce from the rich farmlands of the steppe, and giant crayfish caught by divers on the river bottom. In true Ukrainian style, we toasted again and again with velvety local vodka to our new friendship, our commonalities, and the Dnieper.

❖   ❖   ❖

Before we boarded a ship to tour the reservoir, we visited the fishermen's flea market. Most of the river's anglers fish with bait on the bottom or with floats for carp and large minnows, tench, perch, and the giant European catfish, or wells. Vendors in the market's shaded stalls offered a vast array of worms, grubs, midge larvae, and special dough concoctions. Tackle selection was also extensive, often homemade, and included ingeniously designed sinkers that bore mesh bags for the placement of chum.

The following week we explored the lower river and estuary, leaving from the dreary port city of Kherson on what appeared to be a 100-foot relic of the former Soviet navy. Heading downstream, we passed rows of funky riverside dachas, or summer cottages, reachable only by boat. They cost, we were told, as little as $300 because they offered scant space for growing vegetables. A brief stop at a fish salting and smoking plant revealed drying racks laden with sea roach—a fish name that would never sell in the United States.

Eventually, we broke out into the open waters of the only slightly saline Black Sea, where fishers from a seafood collective were to demonstrate their techniques. The crew hauled in a large hoop net they had set, and unloaded a bag of hundreds of thrashing, plate-sized bream and a single zander—the European walleye pike. Afterward, we tied our vessels to the mother ship for an open-deck repast and toasted the hardworking fishermen.

That evening we were to visit a field station in the lower river for some recreation and the final meal of the day. This region of the Dnieper is a delta, a bewildering but stunning network of channels lined by tall rush and preserved as a nature sanctuary. As the ship eased its way through the maze, we watched herons and egrets work the shallows, marsh hawks hunt just above the grasses, and terns dive over pods of fish breaking the surface.

It was late when we reached the station, and we were forced to choose between an hour of angling and a sauna. Two of my colleagues, John Boreman and Ike Wirgin, and I opted for the fishing and jumped, with our interpreter, Dimitry Ulianov, into our pair of ancient speedboats. Our guides gunned the boats down the channel to a backwater where the river meets the Black Sea.

Our quarry was redfin, a fish with which we were unfamiliar. We chummed between the water lilies and stands of rush with mean and crushed sunflower seeds and broke out the gear provided: cane poles, handmade quill and cork floats, and earthworms.

Action at the first spot was slow, so the guides paddled the boats to a ten-foot-wide opening in the vegetation on a nearby cul-de-sac that turned out to be brimming with redfin. Our bobbers waddled and then dived under the surface as the hard-to-hook redfin attacked our baits. Not to be confused with the great gamefish of the world, redfin proved to resemble North American golden shiners, but with bright red fins.

It was pure and simple fishing, the kind of sheer fun too many anglers enjoy as children and then outgrow. Even the earnest Dimitry caught the spirit and grabbed the first rod he had held in twenty years, and then proceeded to outfish the rest of us.

A banquet had been laid out on a veranda back at the station, and we feasted on the wealth of the Dnieper — fried zander and bream, bighead carp, crayfish, and caviar, and we drank to fellowship, the river, and the obliging redfin. *(October 5, 1997)*

ABOUT THE CONTRIBUTORS

Pete Bodo has been chasing, catching, shooting, killing, and eating various kinds of fish and game ever since he was old enough to pick up a rock or tie a string to a stick. In addition to his *New York Times* columns, he recently published his first novel, a comic fishing saga, titled *The Trout Whisperers*.

Robert H. Boyle, a special contributor to *Sports Illustrated*, has had a lifelong addiction to fishing that led him to write, among other books, *The Hudson River: A Natural and Unnatural History*, now undergoing revision, and to found Riverkeeper and the Hudson River Foundation for Science and Environmental Research. His latest book, with photographs by his wife, Kathryn, is *Dapping: Flagrante Delicto Fly Fishing with Flies That Fly, Quiver and Jump*.

Patricia Leigh Brown reports for the *New York Times* from San Francisco. She is also a contributing writer for *Architectural Digest* and a lapsed fisherwoman.

Nelson Bryant began writing the "Wood, Field and Stream" column (which later became "Outdoors") for the *New York Times* in 1967 on a full-time basis and continued to do so until he retired a little more than a decade ago. From then until early 2006, he contributed an occasional column as a freelancer.

Bob Butz is an award-winning book author and essayist living in northern Michigan. Butz's most recent book, *Beast of Never, Cat of God: The Search for the Eastern Puma,* in large part got its start from an article he published in the *New York Times* "Outdoors" column in 2001.

C. J. Chivers is a foreign correspondent for the *New York Times,* currently assigned to Moscow. A lifelong fisherman raised in upstate New York, he grew up chasing bass, walleye, pike, perch, trout, salmon, and panfish. He now principally fishes the Atlantic surf for striped bass. He also contributes articles on fishing to *Esquire, Field & Stream,* and *SaltWater Sportsman.*

Adam Clymer, the retired Washington correspondent of the *New York Times,* frequently managed to combine political assignments with trout fishing, winding up with stories in the main and sports sections of the *Times* from such political and fishing hot spots as Montana, Colorado, Iowa, Alaska, and Vermont. Even so, he found that full-time work distracted from serious fishing. Retirement cured that.

James Gorman writes the "Side Effects" column in the *Science Times* and is deputy science editor of the *New York Times.* As a fisherman, he holds what he is certain is a world record: he is the only person ever to have taken a guided float trip on the Madison River during the salmon-fly hatch and gotten skunked.

Paul Guernsey is the editor and associate publisher of *Fly Rod & Reel* magazine. A published novelist as well as a former South American correspondent for the Associated Press, Mr. Guernsey lives on a farm on the coast of Maine with his wife, Maryann, and their two children.

Peter Kaminsky writes about food and the outdoors. His work has appeared in the *New York Times* since 1987. He is the author of numerous books, including *The Moon Pulled Up an Acre of Bass* and *Pig Perfect: Encounters with Remarkable Swine*. He is a frequent contributor to *Food & Wine* and has written extensively for *Field & Stream, Sports Afield*, and *Outdoor Life*.

Nick Karas is an ichthyologist and journalist who writes frequently for newspapers and magazines, including *True, Argosy*, and *Newsday*, where for many years he was the outdoors columnist. He is the author of more than a dozen books, among them *Brook Trout, The Striped Bass*, and two novels, *Hunky* and *The Last Whaler*, which he has just completed.

Verlyn Klinkenborg writes editorials for the *New York Times*. His most recent book is *Timothy; or, Notes of an Abject Reptile*.

Barbara Lloyd was the yachting writer for the *New York Times* from 1984 to 2000. She did a weekly boating column and also covered the America's Cup races in Fremantle, Australia, and San Diego. She also wrote a weekly *Times* ski column for ten winters, and occasionally an "Outdoors" column. She is currently retired, but still writes for the *Times* now and then from her home office in Newport, Rhode Island.

Nick Lyons has been an English professor, a book publisher, a columnist, a book author (of *Spring Creek, Full Creel*, and a dozen others), father of four, and — since before memory — a perfectly lunatic fisherman.

Thomas McGuane was born in Michigan and educated at Michigan State, Yale, and Stanford. He has lived in Montana for the last forty years. McGuane has written fourteen books, including *Gallatin Canyon*, published in July 2006, and *The Longest Silence: A Life in Fishing*.

Ray Ottulich is a New York native and Orvis-endorsed fly-fishing guide who has been fishing since he was twelve. Living for twenty-four years in Montana, he was senior guide at Dave

Blackburn's Kootenai Angler guide service, and helped to pioneer float-fishing on British Columbia's Elk River.

Margot Page first contributed to the *New York Times* "Outdoors" column in 1989. She is the author of three books on sport: *Little Rivers: Tales of a Woman Angler, The Art of Fly Fishing,* and *Just Horses: Living with Horses in America.* She is the granddaughter of the legendary angling writer/editor Sparse Grey Hackle and began her book publishing career working with Nick Lyons Books in 1984. Now a freelance book editor and writer/researcher, she lives in Vermont.

James Prosek has been contributing to the *New York Times* "Outdoors" column as a writer and illustrator since 2000. He is the author of seven books and the recipient of a Peabody Award for a documentary he wrote, co-produced, and in which he appeared about the seventeenth-century author Izaak Walton and his book *The Compleat Angler.* Prosek's eighth book and first novel, *The Day My Mother Left,* will be published in spring 2007. He is also working on a book about eels.

Stephen Sautner has contributed to the *New York Times* "Outdoors" column since 1994. His love of nature began with crabbing expeditions at the Jersey Shore with his parents and two brothers. He works for the Bronx Zoo–based Wildlife Conservation Society, where he publicizes the society's international conservation programs.

Ernest Schwiebert is one of America's best-known angling writers, the author of such seminal works as *Trout* and *Matching the Hatch.* Though he earned two doctorate degrees from Princeton University, he gave up a career in architecture in 1977 largely to go fishing. He died in 2005 at age seventy-four.

Ken Schultz is the fishing editor and featured columnist for ESPNOutdoors.com. His new book, *Bass Madness: Bigmouths,*

Big Money, and Big Dreams at the Bassmaster Classic, was published in October 2006. He was formerly fishing editor and for three decades a staff writer for *Field & Stream,* and a commentator for ESPN's *BassCenter.* Inducted into the Freshwater Fishing Hall of Fame in 1998, he is the author of seventeen books on sportfishing and travel topics, including the highly praised bible of recreational fishing, *Ken Schultz's Fishing Encyclopedia and Worldwide Angling Guide.*

Craig Springer's early experiences hunting and fishing near Oxford, Ohio, course through him still. Smallmouth bass made a lasting impression, leading to an M.S. in fisheries science and a career with the U.S. Fish & Wildlife Service. He's also earned an M.A. in rhetoric and writing, studying the rhetoric of conservation, nature, and the outdoors. He lives in New Mexico with his wife, Felicia, and two young anglers, Carson and Willow.

Dave Taft, a New York City native, began exploring the natural world in Canarsie, where he and his brother learned to snare, bottle, shoot, capture, collect, and/or trap bugs, crabs, fish, rocks, shells, reptiles, birds, worms, and other small unfortunates. He presently works as the district ranger for the Jmaica Bay Wildlife Refuge, where he snares, bottles, shoots, captures, and studies bugs, crabs, fish, rocks, shells, and worms for the National Park Service. His illustrations have also graced the pages of the "Outdoors" column over the past fifteen years.

Greg Thomas's work has appeared in all the major sporting periodicals, and he has written five books on fly-fishing, including *Fly Fisher's Bible: Montana.* He is the managing editor of *Big Sky Journal* and lives in Ennis, Montana, with his wife, Becky, daughter, Tate, and a Labrador retriever named Moose.

John van Vliet has been a contributor to the *New York Times* since 2002. He is the author of more than half a dozen books on fly-fishing, including the best-selling *The Art of Fly Tying*. He lives in St. Paul, Minnesota.

John Waldman is a recently appointed professor of biology at Queens College of the City University of New York, following a twenty-year career at the Hudson River Foundation for Science and Environmental Research. His research interests grew from a childhood spent exploring the "wild" shores of the East Bronx. He published his first "Outdoors" column in 1983, and has written and edited popular books on New York Harbor, marine phenomena, striper fishing, and odd ways of catching fish. He lives with his wife, Carol, children Laura and Steve, boats, and fishing gear in Sea Cliff, Long Island, and West Cornwall, Connecticut.

ACKNOWLEDGMENTS

This anthology could not have been possible without the tireless work of Susan B. Adams, formerly of the *New York Times* sports department, who served as editor, chief cook, and bottle washer of the "Outdoors" column for more than two decades. Without her endless enthusiasm and encouragement, some of us may have chosen to write about golf or mountain climbing. And of course thanks to all of my fellow columnists for deciding to write about fishing, especially Nelson Bryant, whose columns inspired many of us to submit our first stories. Thanks also to John Glusman of Harmony Books and Peter McGuigan of Sanford J. Greenburger Associates. If it weren't for them, this collection might reside only in a dusty archive.

Dery Bennett, John Waldman, and Richard Reagan, besides being fine fishing partners, gave valuable input — sometimes between casts — on how the columns should be organized. I'd also like to acknowledge my friends and colleagues at the Bronx Zoo–based Wildlife Conservation Society, which saves wildlife and wild lands — coincidentally near some of the best fishing holes on earth. Finally, thanks to my oldest brother for losing that big fluke off the fishing pier at Long Beach Island in 1978. I'm still trying to catch it.